Every Day with

Jesus

SEP/OCT 20

C000293726

Waverley Abbey Resources is the operating name of CWR: CWR, Waverley Abbey House, Waverley Lane, Farnham, Surrey GU9 8EP, UK Tel: 01252 784700

Email: mail@waverleyabbey.org Registered Charity No. 294387. Registered Limited Company No. 1990308.

Where possible, every effort has been made to ensure that these devotional notes contain the correct permissions and references. Please contact the Publisher directly for any further permissions information.

Cover image: Adobe Stock

Printed in the UK by Bishops Printers

WAVERLEY ABBEY
RESOURCES

MIX
Paper from
responsible sources
FSC® C015900

Every Day with Jesus is available in large print from Waverley Abbey Resources. It is also available on **audio** and **DAISY** in the UK and Eire for the sole use of those with a visual impairment worse than N12, or who are registered blind. For details please contact **Torch Trust for the Blind**, Tel: 01858 438260. Torch House, Torch Way, Northampton Road, Market Harborough LE16 9HL.

1 Thessalonians 5:12–18
**'Rejoice always, pray continually, give thanks in all circumstances;
for this is God's will for you in Christ Jesus.'** (vv16–18)

A fresh edition of *EDWJ*. Over the next two months we shall be looking at giving thanks to God. Paul here associates giving thanks with both prayer and the changing circumstances of our lives.

September is the start of autumn in Britain. We anticipate fierce storms. Heavy rains can saturate the soil, and strong winds bring down trees whose roots are weakened in sodden ground. Great, centuries-old oaks can be felled in a moment, ending life as horizontal skeletons stretched out across our landscape. Walking along woodland paths the morning after the great storm of 1987 meant clambering across felled lumber that resembled a woodland graveyard.*

Such evidence reveals that it's not how strong you appear but how deep your roots grow that determines stability and endurance. And this is true of our Christian lives. It is in giving thanks to God and through continuous prayer that we nourish our Christian roots, so that we remain rooted, even as we are battered and shaken.

We can expect the unexpected throughout our lives, for our enemy prowls around waiting to consume us (1 Pet. 5:8). But in such situations, like the prophet Habakkuk, we are to focus on God rather than our feelings or circumstances. God can give us a perspective that enables us to persevere through our struggles.

RELATED SCRIPTURE TO CONSIDER: Hab. 1:1–4; 2:1; 3:17–19; Psa. 46; Jer. 17:7–9; Col. 2:6–12.

AN ACTION TO TAKE: What helps you to grow deeper roots in Christ? Where is there a danger that you might be uprooted by a fierce and unexpected storm?

A PRAYER TO MAKE: 'Lord, thank You that I am rooted in You and Your word. May I daily seek to become more firmly rooted in Your truth. Amen.'

Write to **micha@edwj.org** with your stories and questions and I'll write back in confidence as soon as I can.

*countryfile.com/people/experiences/the-great-storm-of-1987-what-happened-and-how-did-it-change-weather-forecasting/

Psalm 89:1–4
**'I will declare that your love stands firm for ever, that you
have established your faithfulness in heaven itself.'** (v2)

Paul, writing to the Corinthian church, states that 'love never fails'
(1 Cor. 13:8a). Unfailing love can and will outlast everything. A
church as fragmented as that in Corinth needed to heed his
reminder to express such love.

Today, our model is Jesus, who emptied Himself to live on earth
and whose love did not fail throughout all the agonies of injustice and
execution He experienced. In moments of intense pressure, we need both
to know the reality of, and invest our hope in, the unfailing love of God.

We seldom go to bed imagining that whilst asleep the world will
radically change. There is some comfort in the regular rhythms offered
by the seasons. Indeed, we navigate our days by the celebrations that
mark out our year. Such rhythms give order and confidence to our
daily lives.

When such rhythms are broken, through the loss of a loved one
or the terror of a global pandemic, we can experience a rapid rise
in stress. It's important, therefore, to remind ourselves of God's
permanent and unfailing love, even as we feel blown this way and that
by forces beyond our control. In it we discover the strength to go on.

This is why we declare our confidence in God's never failing
presence each and every day. Our verbal affirmation resonates
throughout creation in affirmation of the Lord of the universe.

RELATED SCRIPTURE TO CONSIDER: 1 Kings 4:29–34; Psa. 62:1–8; Luke 1:46–55;
1 Cor. 2:1–10.

AN ACTION TO TAKE: Establish daily rhythms with God, in your prayer and Bible
encounter, for only by standing on the rock, who is Christ, will we endure
uncertain times (Matt. 7:24–29).

A PRAYER TO MAKE: 'Lord, in peace we shall lie down and sleep, for You alone
make us dwell in safety. Amen.'*

*Night Prayer from, Society of St Francis, *Celebrating Common Prayer. Pocket Version* (London: Mowbray,
1998).

Psalm 89:14–18

'Blessed are those who have learned to acclaim you, who walk in the light of your presence, LORD.' (v15)

The word 'acclaim' actually means 'to cry out to'. We are people who have hopefully become familiar with crying out to God. In joy or despondency, we are invited to direct our first words towards God, for God is both the source and the solution in our delight and in our desolation.

God accompanies us every step, every day. We are continually in God's presence and, as such, can continuously listen to and talk with Him, the very essence of our prayer. Whilst we may set aside specific times for prayer, talking with God throughout our day is a good habit to establish.

I have a prayer, taken from the Orthodox tradition, that provides me with ten short phrases that I have spread across my day. I am now familiar with them and so they are landmarks within the uncertain terrain of daily life. Familiarity provokes my heart to rise towards God as my lips acclaim God, my ever-present help in trouble (Psa. 46:1).

There are also great acclamations in the Psalms; such as, 'Oh Lord open my lips, and my mouth will declare your praise' (Psa. 51:15, ESV). These offer excellent walking declarations; I breathe in on the first part of the verse, breath out on the second. Every step is a declaration of my confidence in God and builds faith.

In this way, we learn continuously to walk in the light of God's presence (Psa. 89:15b). Certainly one way we can improve our everyday walk with Jesus.

RELATED SCRIPTURE TO CONSIDER: 1 Sam. 1:1–18; Psa. 45:1–2; John 17; Acts 7:48–60.

AN ACTION TO TAKE: Familiarise yourself with verses from the Psalms and recite them as you journey through your day; for example, 'My help comes from the LORD, the Maker of heaven and earth' (Psa. 121:2).

A PRAYER TO MAKE: 'Lord, help me in all things to rely upon Your holy will. Amen.'

Psalm 1

**'but whose delight is in the law of the LORD, and
who meditates on his law day and night.'** (v2)

In all honesty, it's taken a while for me to find delight in God's Word.
Indeed, early on in my Christian life, my quiet time was endurance
more than enjoyment. Instructed as a new Christian to read my
Bible and pray, I dutifully did so. Bible notes, then the Salvation Army's
The Soldier's Armoury, were my essential diet. I was learning to grasp
my need for God's bread of life.

Delight means complete satisfaction, and even today there are many
things that compete with Scripture when it comes to seeking personal
satisfaction. However, reading Scripture means encountering God, for
it is the bread of life, it feeds us (Matt. 4:4).

The Bible can prove difficult to understand, but offers us the space to
meet with God. For our encouragement, the Church has chosen to live
under the Bible's authority, and we can all find faith, hope and love by
taking time to read it.

The psalmist reminds us that we are to meditate on God's law
continuously and wrestle with understanding what we read. In doing
so, we identify points of resistance within us. At such points, we're
prompted to see life as our journey of self-surrender, one that presents
us with a simple choice; God's way or my way? After 48 years of
following Jesus, I surprise myself how often I remain resistant to self-
surrender.

RELATED SCRIPTURE TO CONSIDER: Psa. 119:1–8; Prov. 2:1–15;
Matt. 4:1–11; John 6:1–59.

AN ACTION TO TAKE: There are many ways to engage with the Bible. One way is
to learn through greater study. I recommend Waverley Abbey's three-year
course in 'Search the Scriptures'. Go at your own pace and discover the
wisdom in God's Word edwj.org/so21-4sep

A PRAYER TO MAKE: 'Lord, teach me through Your Word daily and help me to live
every day with Jesus. Amen.'

New releases from Waverley Abbey Resources

The Bird Who Sang Again

Your life sings to those around you. Judy Moore will inspire you to sing out the messages you were designed to carry, and tell the story you have been uniquely crafted to tell.

Strengthen Your Core

Have you felt a little sluggish in your spiritual practices? Are you yearning for spiritual growth, but you're not too sure how to get there? This book will kickstart your spiritual training regime. In eight workouts for your soul, you'll be roused into action and spurred into your spiritual growth spurt.

The God Files Bible

This colourfully presented Bible – in which each book is styled as a 'file' – will invite children into the story of Scripture by encouraging them to play their part as agents with a mission, inspired by the adventures and impact of the special agents they read about, such as Joseph, David, Esther and Mary.

To find out more about all our new releases, visit
waverleyabbeyresources.org/category/new-releases/

Psalm 118
'The Lord has done it this very day; let us rejoice today and be glad.' (v24)

Steadfast love is something we yearn for deep within. It offers complete acceptance and affirmation. It does not excuse our bad behaviour or mistakes, but offers a precious moment to address their consequences. It's a place of safety, where wounds are licked, lessons learned, and a fresh start made.

This is the place God invites us to enter every day, and frequently throughout each day, as we stumble through life – both with fresh challenges and as we deal with the baggage that we carry from our past (from our own sins and where we've been the victim of another's offence).

Sunday – for Christians the first day of the week, celebrating Christ's resurrection – offers a great time for reflection on the week just past. I like to build time each Sunday, before attending a church gathering, quietly to consider my past week.

This offers a regular, simple space for some honesty with God and with myself. I can face up to disappointments without self-pity but honestly acknowledge my human frailty. Set against God's compassionate and enduring love, I then refocus, make adjustments, and renew my commitment to honour God, learning from the substance of my reflections.

Worshipping a compassionate God is something I regularly give thanks for. Regardless of my mistakes, God consistently welcomes me back into His presence.

RELATED SCRIPTURE TO CONSIDER: Lev. 5:1–13; Psa. 32; James 4:7–10; 1 John 1:5–10.

AN ACTION TO TAKE: Identify a suitable time each Sunday for such a reflection of your past week. Make this a time where you enjoy God's steadfast love.

A PRAYER TO MAKE: 'Lord, thank You that I can have confidence to approach You and take comfort from Your enduring love. Amen.' (Heb. 4:16)

Romans 1:8–15

"First, I thank my God through Jesus Christ for all of you, because your faith is being reported all over the world.' (v8)

It was always something of a trial writing thank you letters after Christmas. My parents insisted. I was grateful for my presents, but had little desire to sit down and put pen to paper. I only wanted to play with my gifts, with little appreciation for the love and sacrifice of those who'd supplied my presents. My enjoyment had been conceived by them long before I enjoyed the pleasure myself. Something I now understand as I seek to find presents for those I love.

It is all too easy to separate the gift from the giver. We can assume that the confidence we find in God, the encouragement we take from church gatherings, is something we can expect and assume is ours by right. Yet, much of our Christian experience is built upon the variety of contributions made by other Christians.

All too easily we become consumed with our own experience, and fail to give thanks for what we owe to the investment of others in providing that moment of insight, reassurance or help. A consumer is defined as, 'a person who buys goods or services for their own use'.* Our God encounters are freely given, yet often through the kind endeavours of others. Like Paul, let's take time to give thanks for those, known and unknown, who continue to contribute to encouraging us in our faith.

RELATED SCRIPTURE TO CONSIDER: Exod. 17:8–13; Lev. 19:9–18; Rom. 12:3–21; Phil. 2:1–11.

AN ACTION TO TAKE: Starting with prayer for those who have encouraged us, we might also think of dropping a card, even a small gift, into the hands of those we are truly grateful to.

A PRAYER TO MAKE: 'Lord, thank You that I am incapable of sustaining my Christian life on my own, but I am a beneficiary of the love and faithful service of so many fellow Christians. Amen.'

*dictionary.cambridge.org/dictionary/english/consumer [accessed 01.05/2021]

1 Corinthians 1:4–9

'For in him you have been enriched in every way – with all kinds of speech and with all knowledge – God thus confirming our testimony about Christ among you. Therefore you do not lack any spiritual gift as you eagerly wait for our Lord Jesus Christ to be revealed.' (vv5–7)

I am grateful we live in an age in which we have at our fingertips a vast resource of Christian wisdom. Where once I had a large library of books, I have been pleased to pass on the majority for the benefit of others because I now enjoy access to the internet.

It is something we can give thanks to God for. We can never say that we are without the tools we need to nurture and grow our faith. It's a privilege at Waverley Abbey to publish physical books, but also increasingly to develop online courses for individuals and groups. People can engage with these at a time and a pace that suits them best.

In the UK, we are in a privileged position of enjoying so much Christian content, yet we are challenged by the apparent decline of the Christian population. Our great challenge is to avoid simply putting on spiritual weight, whilst failing to share the treasure trove so easily available and accessible to everyone hungering for truth.

I'm thrilled that my daughter has a pile of *Every Day With Jesus* booklets in her design studio and that many of those visiting walk away with a copy and tell her how helpful they prove to be. We never know where people will find the wisdom and insight they are seeking.

The purpose of our Christian faith is not to accumulate greater knowledge of Jesus for our own sake but to share God's love and kindness with everyone we meet. So, let's give thanks for the living Word of God who expresses Himself through our lives as we interact with others every day.

RELATED SCRIPTURE TO CONSIDER: Zech. 7; Prov. 3:27–35; Col. 2:4–6; James 3:13–18.

AN ACTION TO TAKE: *EDWJ* is a great way to introduce someone to God. Who can you give a copy of *EDWJ* to? Order some additional copies and set yourself the target to give them away each month.

A PRAYER TO MAKE: 'Lord, You are 'the way, the truth and the life' for everyone. Show me how I can encourage my friends to encounter God. Amen.'

Consolation

2 Corinthians 1:1–7

'Who comforts us in all our troubles, so that we can comfort those in any trouble with the comfort we ourselves receive from God.' (v4)

This appears to be a strange greeting and not something for which we might consider giving thanks. After all, who amongst us wants to pass through the suffering of affliction? Yet, it seems, even as Christians, we cannot avoid pain in life.

Creatively, what we learn through our sufferings can become the source of encouragement and enable others to anticipate and navigate their own course though life's setbacks. Whilst we are not to assume the worst of life, we shall all encounter an unanticipated crisis, usually more than one.

Whilst stressful, perhaps one important way to approach and endure such episodes is to seek to discover how our experience might become a source of encouragement and consolation to others. Such stories offer hope when all we had imagined disintegrates before us, and we must find the resolve to continue with a life far removed from that we had expected.

In this way, following the example left us by Jesus' life and passion, the Church has built up a narrative on human resilience and how we can find the courage and ability to bounce forward, regardless of limitations that are not of our own choosing. We find a measure of consolation, and with it fresh capacity to continue our journey of faith with God and alongside each other, even as we are saddened and challenged through our experience.

RELATED SCRIPTURE TO CONSIDER: Psa. 119:49–64; Isa. 53; Rom. 5:1–11; 8:18–30.

AN ACTION TO TAKE: If you are looking at how you might bounce forwards, read Patrick Regan's book of that name **edwj.org/so21-8sep**

A PRAYER TO MAKE: 'Lord, may I find Your consolation within my suffering and offer encouragement to others struggling with life's challenges. Amen.'

Gal. 1:1–5
**'Grace and peace to you from God our Father
and the Lord Jesus Christ'**(v3).

One of the great insights I have drawn from the Gospels is Jesus' commitment to 'truth telling'. Some years ago, the media adopted a phrase regarding political pronouncements. They described politicians as being, 'economical with the truth'. In other words, carefully constructing words to reveal only so much of the reality that they wanted the public to know.

The good news in the Bible is that Jesus tells it straight. From it I know my own condition outside of Christ, the practical consequences of sin, which is failing to walk in God's way, and how to manage my relationships with others. It's the best guidebook for navigating life.

At the start of his letter to the Galatians, in which Paul engages in some tough talk over social and cultural compromise, he declares his honest ambition for those to whom he writes. He wants this whole difficult conversation to be managed with grace and peace. He means that the conflict isn't to be escalated, thereby deepening the rift, nor are individuals to fail to listen to and hear each other, to communicate effectively.

Truth telling is only ever beneficial when it seeks to serve the interests of another, above my own. Hence, being economical with the truth aims to protect the speaker's integrity. But truth telling seeks to empower the listener to take action, which is in everyone's best interest. This is a further way in which we demonstrate our love for our neighbours.

RELATED SCRIPTURE TO CONSIDER: Exod. 4:1–16; Psa. 107:1–3; John 1:6–14; 1 Cor. 1:10–17.

AN ACTION TO TAKE: Ensure you always think before you speak. Our words can build bridges or create chasms. Will you accept God's invitation to be a bridge builder?

A PRAYER TO MAKE: 'Lord, help me to speak truth with love, always with the interests of the one whom I am talking to in mind. Amen.'

Eph. 1:1–10

'Praise be to the God and Father of our Lord Jesus Christ, who has blessed us in the heavenly realms with every spiritual blessing in Christ.' (v3)

'When you are discouraged, thinking all is lost, Count your many blessings, name them one by one, And it will surprise you what the Lord has done.'* These lyrics were penned by Johnson Oatman Jr, and perhaps offer the inspiration behind what has grown into gratitude journalling.

There is increasing scientific evidence that adopting a gratitude attitude to life is good for our health and wellbeing.** Yet, it's something that the followers of Jesus have always known. Taking time to reflect upon the many ways God sustains and encourages us is an exercise which will pay dividends when we hit the buffers.

Throughout church history, many have written of the depths of despondency into which the human heart can sink. In such moments, it's no good just giving oneself a motivational talk. Emotionally, psychologically and physically, life becomes an endurance race, one in which I'm no longer sure I want to compete.

When facing such days myself, what I call 'blue mood days', I do begin to count my blessings. I can only manage these one at a time as I wrestle within with disappointment, even personal despair. Yet, they are like handholds that will inevitably lead me back to God. Whilst I might argue internally over their reality, they remain the stepping stones that will ultimately lead me back into God's warm embrace.

RELATED SCRIPTURE TO CONSIDER: 1 Chron. 16:7–36; Psa. 28:6–9; Phil. 4:4–13; Col. 2:6–10.

AN ACTION TO TAKE: Make a note of the things you are grateful for. You can revisit this list on a 'blue mood day'.

A PRAYER TO MAKE: 'Lord, may I take time daily to identify those things for which I am grateful; Your blessings in my life. Amen.'

*hymnologyarchive.com/count-your-blessings [accessed 05/05/2021]
**positivepsychology.com/benefits-of-gratitude [accessed 05/05/2021]

Philippians 1:1–6
'I thank my God every time I remember you. In all my prayers for all of you, I always pray with joy because of your partnership in the gospel from the first day until now' (vv3–5)

Everyone praying and working at Waverley Abbey is encouraged to know we are not alone. Our global *Every Day With Jesus* readership is praying and working with us, which puts a spring in our step as we present the gospel. Together we serve as ambassadors of hope to a vulnerable, and often troubled, world.

This message of hope was one demonstrated by Jesus. He revealed the heart of heaven as He came alongside individuals with a challenge to live God's way in difficult circumstances (John 4:1–26). Jesus calls us to direct our attention to encouraging and supporting others.

Sadly, throughout its long history, God's Church has invested far too much time and energy in criticising others. The consequent and numerous church splits confirm that the love we speak of is so often only skin deep. It proves insufficiently resilient to ride out differences of perspective. One of the major criticisms of the Church remains its inability to express Christian solidarity.

Partnership means that I choose to encourage everyone to learn to live every day with Jesus. Disagreements will remain, but there will be a consensus around the life, death and resurrection of Christ. Without such there can be no true transformation. With it, we can work together to change the world. Let's agree to keep that as our primary aim.

RELATED SCRIPTURE TO CONSIDER: Luke 7:1–50; John 13:31–38; Acts 2:37–47.

AN ACTION TO TAKE: Consider ordering in copies of *EDWJ* to share with friends as we partner together in the gospel. We also offer Inspiring Women Every Day (IWED) as a free resource.

A PRAYER TO MAKE: 'Lord, help me to build up the body of Christ rather than tear it down with my criticism. Amen.'

Write to **micha@edwj.org** with your stories and questions and I'll write back in confidence as soon as I can.

Sacrifice of Praise

Hebrews 13:11–16

'Through Jesus, therefore, let us continually offer to God a sacrifice of praise – the fruit of lips that openly profess his name.' (v15)

Every time I carry rubbish out to the dustbin I consider the love and grace of God. For I have continually to place my life's garbage into the hands of the eternal rubbish collector. Just as I accumulate rubbish throughout my week ahead of the bin collection, so too I create a constant stream of waste from which I need God's cleansing grace. We can all give thanks that in the activities of daily life we can discern the face and purpose of God.

There are times when giving thanks costs us something. Perhaps overwhelmed by immediate circumstances, we find it hard to reach for any authentic words of praise. Yet, Jesus did not find it easy to go willingly to the cross (Matt. 26:39). All sacrifice requires that we give up something. It costs us, and giving thanks will often carry a price tag.

Corrie ten Boom, reflecting on her experiences in a concentration camp, reminds us, 'When a train goes through a tunnel and it gets dark, you don't throw away the ticket and jump off. You sit still and trust the engineer.'* It's not our situation for which we offer thanks, it is the one who accompanies us in our situation that we praise.

Jesus Himself was taken outside Jerusalem and crucified on a garbage heap. God can always be found in the accumulated rubbish of our lives.

RELATED SCRIPTURE TO CONSIDER: Ezra 3; Psa. 103:1–6; Matt. 24:3–14; Acts 14:19–28.

AN ACTION TO TAKE: How might you integrate your friendship with God into the everyday tasks that make up your day? This is how we can practise to walk the talk.

A PRAYER TO MAKE: 'Lord, may I give You thanks in the difficult, as well as the good, times. Amen.'

* brainyquote.com/quotes/corrie_ten_boom_393675, [accessed 07/05/2021]

Ecclesiastes 1:12–18
**'For with much wisdom comes much sorrow; the
more knowledge, the more grief.'** (v18)

Knowledge and wisdom are different. Knowledge is the
understanding we gain from study and experience; wisdom is
learning the skills to put that knowledge to work. It is wisdom that
guides us in making good decisions from our knowledge.

As disciples we need both. Our knowledge of God gives us an
understanding of who God is and what God requires, whilst wisdom
enables us to apply it to our lives. Indeed, most people want to know
how God works in practice, rather than further facts about God.

Jayne knows God loves her; the Bible says so. But how can she make
sense of that love when her body is full of pain? The acute nature of
that pain distracts her from settling in for a Bible study; she struggles
to stay comfortable in any one position for more than ten minutes.

Instantly, many of the normal ways we engage with God are placed
beyond her reach. Yet, her knowledge of God's abiding presence has
given her the wisdom to find ways within her physical limitations to
encounter God in prayer. She has found forms of prayer that operate
effectively within the persistent pressure and sorrow of her discomfort.

That's why Jayne led our Waverley Abbey Retreat on finding Christ in
the wilderness of chronic pain. A space that drew those who similarly
battle daily with their pain, yet also love and serve God. We can be
grateful for the diversity of knowledge, experience and rich wisdom
throughout God's Church.

RELATED SCRIPTURE TO CONSIDER: 2 Chron. 20:1–17; Eccl. 1:1–11; Matt. 5:1–13;
2 Cor. 6:1–10.

AN ACTION TO TAKE: Acknowledge what sorrows are troubling you. How might
you discover God within such sorrows? Are you able to worship God within
the storm?

A PRAYER TO MAKE: 'Lord, help me to turn my gaze from the source of my sorrow
and direct it towards You. Amen.'

Righteous Living

Ecclesiastes 2:17–26

'To the person who pleases him, God gives wisdom, knowledge and happiness, but to the sinner he gives the task of gathering and storing up wealth to hand it over to the one who pleases God. This too is meaningless, a chasing after the wind.' (v26).

To an external observer, the life of the righteous and unrighteous look much the same. We are not privy to their private thoughts and misdemeanours. Yet, they both navigate their day in a similar way. Rising to go to work and returning home to rest, one day gives way to the next with very little variance.

Some question the value of righteous living, as it appears to carry an equal amount of pain and sorrow as the unrighteous (Matt. 5:45). However, the distinction lies within the lens through which we choose to view life.

In our pursuit of God, we have access to a broad understanding of the purpose of life itself. More than that, our brief mortal sojourn is a small, if significant, part of our eternal destiny. Such a perspective can only ever be sustained by faith, one that is the product of knowledge and its offspring, wisdom.

Life presents hardships. We can choose to wrestle with these and moan about our fate, growing increasingly despondent. Or, we can nurture the hope deposited within our heart by God's Spirit and choose to endure with a confidence that God is all and in all (Eph. 4:4–6). Faith is a muscle in need of continuous exercise – it might just be that we need to start a fresh workout.

RELATED SCRIPTURE TO CONSIDER: Psa. 22:1–11; Hab. 2:1–5; 1 Cor. 3:1–15; Eph. 4:7–16.

AN ACTION TO TAKE: If it's time to start a new workout, pick up a copy of Jenny Campbell's newly published *Strengthen Your Core: Practical Spiritual Formation for Every Day* **edwj.org/so21-14sep**

A PRAYER TO MAKE: 'Lord, may I remind myself continually that I am here to glorify and enjoy You forever. Amen.''

'Westminster Shorter Catechism: apuritansmind.com/westminster-standards/shorter-catechism/ [accessed 08/05/2021]

Ecclesiastes 3:9–14

**'He has made everything beautiful in its time. He has also
set eternity in the human heart; yet no one can fathom
what God has done from beginning to end.'**(v11)

Grasping God and His ways lies well beyond the capacity of our human understanding. We wrestle too often with the question, 'Why?' Certainly, this is the question that most often unsettles us: 'Why did my relationship end?' 'Why did I lose my job?' 'Why did I do what I knew was wrong?'

There is seldom a satisfactory answer. God invites us to turn inward and consider the seed of eternity planted within our heart. Whilst mortality comes with its own expiration date, unknown yet unavoidable, we carry within us the seed of purpose that flourishes throughout eternity. Death merely offers the threshold beyond which we enter into the fullness of our redemption.

True faith is revealed in our resilience to reframe our life experience against that backdrop of eternity. This won't shield us from life's painful realities, yet will empower us to live with our face uplifted within all such harsh realities (Acts 7:55–56). Indeed, such experiences present opportunities from within which a window may be opened into God's kingdom.

It is in learning to discover God in the unremitting, unexciting details of daily life that trains us to reflect the life of God in our thoughts, words and deeds. Life provokes us, and we respond either in ways that reveal God to a watching world, or that question the viability of our Christian proclamation.

RELATED SCRIPTURE TO CONSIDER: Isa. 43:1–7; Dan. 6:1–23; 1 Tim. 6:6–16; 1 Pet. 1:3–9.

AN ACTION TO TAKE: Seek to find creative ways to look beyond the immediate situation and focus upon the seed of eternity planted within your own heart.

A PRAYER TO MAKE: 'Lord, when situations are beyond my understanding, may I be content to entrust myself to Your care. Amen.'

Active Listening

Ecclesiastes 5:1–7

'Do not be quick with your mouth, do not be hasty in your heart to utter anything before God. God is in heaven and you are on earth, so let your words be few.' (v2)

Talking is too easy. We have phrases such as 'stop digging', indicating the more we speak the more we incriminate ourselves. Chatter, in both verbal and written form, threatens to overwhelm us. From podcasts to tweets, we are surrounded by the free expression of opinions, yet with little time to digest what's being said.

The roots of the word 'listen' are to hear and obey. Approaching God, we all too often fill the airwaves with our voice, failing to pause to listen to the Lord of the universe.

Relationships grow from two-way communication. We learn about another person's preferences and discover more about ourselves. This is the heartbeat of prayer. Taking time with God, I learn who I am from God's perspective.

Yet silence is often intimidating. Left alone, we discover how uncomfortable we are in our own skin. We quickly seek to drown out the silence with sounds; builders have radios blaring, we click on the TV rather than enjoy a few moments of quiet. So many struggle with silence.

I remain grateful for periods of silence. My day starts with 20 minutes of silence. My car is a haven of silence, with the radio always turned off. For it is in the silence that we hear the whisper of God; a whisper that inspires, encourages and comforts in equal measure.

RELATED SCRIPTURE TO CONSIDER: 1 Kings 19:1–13; Jonah 1:1–10; Mark 6:30–32, 45–52; Acts 10:9–23.

AN ACTION TO TAKE: It is impossible to stop the distraction noise creates in our lives instantly. Try developing a habit of taking 15 minutes, somewhere in your day, just to be silent and still.

A PRAYER TO MAKE: 'Lord, help me to hear Your voice clearly amongst the many voices that demand my attention every day. Amen.'

Ecclesiastes 5:16–20
'Moreover, when God gives someone wealth and possessions, and the ability to enjoy them, to accept their lot and be happy in their toil – this is a gift of God.' (v19)

As disciples, we accept that all that we have comes from God (1 Chron. 29:14). Each of us is invited to live life with our eyes firmly fixed upon God. However, it's so easy to be distracted by the appetites that stir within us, from greed to lust. Whilst our inner appetites, as the Church Fathers described them, easily motivate us, it is God's Spirit who can mobilise us to live at peace with God, ourselves and our neighbours.

In our pursuit of inner peace we may explore many disciplines. Yet, Scripture reminds us that contentment is found in God alone (John 10:10). Learning to find contentment in the life we find ourselves living is indeed a gift of God. In many ways, it flies in the face of the superficial message society seeks to communicate: That the ideal life is pain free and financially underwritten. Yet, few enjoy such a life. We don't celebrate pain or frugality; however, we discover that God occupies our greatest nightmares as completely as our fantasies.

Certainly I have failed many times in 'accepting my lot'. I have reacted, been disgruntled, angry and embittered. However, I only rob myself. Straining to set myself free, my struggles only deepen my despondency, whilst I lose sight of God, and all too easily blame God, making Him the scapegoat for all my troubles.

RELATED SCRIPTURE TO CONSIDER: 1 Chron. 29:1–20; Psa. 74; Rom. 11:33–12:2; James 1:1–17.

AN ACTION TO TAKE: Where do you struggle to live at peace with God and yourself? It is here that you are invited to seek and find God.

A PRAYER TO MAKE: 'Lord, may I give thanks every day for the life I have entrusted to You, and may I live with both eyes focused on You alone. Amen.'

Invest in your mental health and wellbeing

Learn online, at your own pace, and gain greater knowledge to better understand yourself and others.

Would you like to feel better equipped at supporting friends or family through difficult times? Perhaps you'd like some guidance to understand your own mental health or wellbeing challenges.

Whether you're going through a blip, or supporting somebody who is, these courses will help you understand how and why some people are affected in these areas. Through the Insight learning platform, you'll discover the value of a healthy mindset and ways to navigate challenges.

Insight into Anxiety

Anxiety affects many people today. Explore key issues with anxiety, and skills and strategies to manage and overcome it. This course offers insight for those who want to help others, as well as those who face issues with anxiety themselves.

Insight into Self-Esteem

This 4 session course will lead you through an exploration of the importance of self esteem and how as Christians it is rooted in our relationship with God.

To find out more about our Insight courses please visit

waverleyabbeyresources.org/insight

A Good Name

Ecclesiastes 7:1–6
**'A good name is better than fine perfume, and the
day of death better than the day of birth.'** (v1)

Setting priorities is an imperative. As a youngster, I saw time endlessly stretching out before me. As I have aged, so the speed with which time passes has increased, and my endgame comes into ever-clearer focus.

An awareness of our mortality will immediately intensify our awareness of God, or the void that exists where God fits best. All too often it is the challenging events that threaten our very existence that serve as catalysts to focus our attention upon God.

In setting our priorities it's worth asking how best might we be remembered. For some, it is in the nature of their so-called legacy; for others, in the scale of their measurable achievements. Nothing wrong with either. However, the challenge I think Scripture places before us is the degree to which a deposit of God is left on this earth.

One of my favourite verses is, 'Enoch walked faithfully with God; then he was no more, because God took him away' (Gen. 5:24). We discover that as we devote ourselves to living every day with Jesus, it is God's fragrance and truth that is expressed through our life. So often, it's only my own momentary whims that people carry away with them. Then all they encounter is my fractured mortality. A missed opportunity to have lived as God's witness. This is perhaps my greatest disappointment as I consider my daily walk of faith.

RELATED SCRIPTURE TO CONSIDER: Josh. 24:1–18; Deut. 6:1–12; 1 Cor. 10:23–33; 1 Pet. 3:13–22.

AN ACTION TO TAKE: In what ways might you prioritise walking with Jesus every day so that God's good name is indeed the scent that perfumes your life and impacts others?

A PRAYER TO MAKE: 'Lord, help me like Enoch to become an expression of God's grace in my life and work, so it is You alone who is seen. Amen.'

Ecclesiastes 7:8–9
**'The end of a matter is better than its beginning,
and patience is better than pride.'** (v8)

My many years serving as a mediator gave me the privilege of being brought into diverse disputes. From commercial disagreements to relational breakdown, most people are captured by their past and present, rather than their future.

Ending well is something Jesus illustrates perfectly. Yielding to His call and refusing to be bated by the insults of His enemies or the disappearance of His friends. Hanging on the cross, He calls upon His Father to forgive all who reject Him, even though they casually get on with their own lives, still ignoring the suffering servant (Luke 23:34).

Jesus was incarnate for the long game, turning a lost people back to God and re-establishing friendship forever. Obviously there was a need to recognise and repent of past faults, yet the reason was never for what lay behind but for as yet unrealised possibilities.

Too often, past and present experiences can blind us to tomorrow's opportunities. We find ourselves making little progress along perpetual cul-de-sacs because we've failed to consider the nature of the context in which we find ourselves. Mediators speak of 'win-win outcomes', reminding conflicted parties that there is a price attached. Jesus knew the price tag – and paid it. Will we respond and live for all the future opportunities available to us within the conflicts we face, both internal and external?

RELATED SCRIPTURE TO CONSIDER: Psa. 32; Isa. 44:21–23; Matt. 5:21–26; 6:5–15.

AN ACTION TO TAKE: Are there unresolved issues that disturb your peace of mind? Ask God how you might best respond and let go of the past to take hold of your future.

A PRAYER TO MAKE: 'Lord, forgive me, and in owning my past, help me to walk into my future hand in hand with You. Amen.'

Ecclesiastes 7:10–14
**'Do not say, "Why were the old days better than these?"
For it is not wise to ask such questions.'** (v10)

Life is a process and, as one generation ages, it perceives that the good old days were better than what they experience today. History teaches that this assumption isn't new or true! Plato recorded Socrates saying, 'The children now love luxury; they have bad manners, contempt for authority; they show disrespect for elders and love chatter in place of exercise'*.

Jesus warns that time is in God's hands, and that we are to attend to our personal discipleship rather than worry about the state of the world (Matt. 24:36-51). It's not that world events don't matter, but they too are subject to God's will and purpose. Our greatest responsibility lies in working out our faith with fear and trembling, whilst praying without ceasing (Phil. 2:12-13 and 1 Thes. 5:17).

It is a joy to consider the tremendous vision of the 'Eternal Wall of Answered Prayer'.** A source of hope, it is a physical reminder of God's grace and goodness throughout history and it preserves that rich Christian heritage of answered prayer. It reminds us that God never fails or forsakes us. It serves as a call for us to return to active prayer in response to God's invitation, and ensures that visitors can discover the truth of the gospel and encounter God for themselves.

Visit their website, look at the advert opposite and commit to pray and recall that the God who answered prayer over the years is still present and powerful today.

RELATED SCRIPTURE TO CONSIDER: Ps. 22:1-11, Obad. 1:11-18, Jas. 4:13-17.

AN ACTION TO TAKE: Take a look at the website of Eternal Wall of Answered Prayer, and recall the ways God has answered your prayers. Send these answers to micha@edwj.org and I will pass them on.

A PRAYER TO MAKE: 'Lord, help me to keep my attention focussed on You alone, and give thanks for Your involvement in my life from my birth. Amen'

* Attributed to SOCRATES by Plato, according to William L. Patty and Louise S. Johnson, Personality and Adjustment, p. 277 (1953). https://www.bartleby.com/73/195.html [accessed 14/05/2021].
** https://www.eternalwall.org.uk/

TOGETHER LET'S
MAKE HOPE VISIBLE

BE PART OF BUILDING THIS LANDMARK OF A MILLION ANSWERED PRAYERS

CROWDFUNDING
13/09/21-22/10/21

eternalwall.org.uk

Human Fracture

Ecclesiastes 7:19–25

'Indeed, there is no one on earth who is righteous, no one who does what is right and never sins.' (v20)

I fear living a self-righteous life – living what I believe, but with a superior attitude that others find offensive. Often, when speaking about God's truth, it's easy to come across as self-righteous.

It's useful to reflect on the fact that we're all fractured people. No one can contribute anything to God's gracious act in setting us free from sin. The time I take criticising another might be better spent considering my own battle with sin and by giving thanks for God's loving acceptance.

The Church can be guilty of appraising sins and attributing a variety of values accordingly. Sadly, sin is the same whether it's lying or murdering. Whilst the consequences may be different in the degree of their impact, the separation from God remains the same.

A dying thief enjoyed God's grace with no time to demonstrate amendment of life (Luke 23:40–43). Restored relationship with God is an act initiated by God alone, one to which we are invited to respond and so lay hold of all salvation's benefits, both now and eternally.

In response to God's great gift, we are invited to consider our own life, rather than criticise someone else. Of course, we are always to seek their best interest, which may be to listen or to offer some practical help. How else will anyone see that God is a God of love, until and unless I live a life born of love; this is to live every day with Jesus.

RELATED SCRIPTURE TO CONSIDER: Num. 20:6–13; Prov. 20:5–12; Luke 18:9–14; Rom. 14.

AN ACTION TO TAKE: How do you practise Jesus' command to love God and your neighbour?

A PRAYER TO MAKE: 'Lord, give me eyes to see people as You see them, and then to pray and support them in finding grace for their lives. Amen.'

Write to **micha@edwj.org** with your stories and questions and I'll write back in confidence as soon as I can.

Ecclesiastes 8:16–17
'No one can comprehend what goes on under the sun. Despite all their efforts to search it out, no one can discover its meaning. Even if the wise claim they know, they cannot really comprehend it.' (v17)

One lesson the Covid pandemic has reinforced is that humanity is a long way from being in charge of its own destiny. For all the scientific and technological advances made through reasoned endeavour, there remain factors which lie well beyond our control. Even though developed nations may have a better chance of managing their impact, the true helplessness of humanity is reflected in those nations where finance and infrastructure cannot be managed to minimise the impact of forces outside of our understanding and control.

Rationality has its place and also its limitations. Comprehending God requires that I step beyond rationality. If God didn't lie outside our rational mind then He couldn't remain omniscient, omnipotent and omnipresent.

What are we to make of circumstances we cannot comprehend? They can either remain a source of anguish or we can entrust them into God's purpose. Lying outside our understanding, they remain the litmus test of our faith. Not an abject surrender but a bold declaration that, despite everything, our God reigns (Psa. 146:1–5).

Resilience requires that we find the resolve to lay hold of the inner resource and external support and encouragement to take the hand life has dealt us and rise to its incomprehensible challenges. Here we find the unique person God created us to become.

RELATED SCRIPTURE TO CONSIDER: Psa. 97; Isa. 52; Matt. 11:25–30; Heb. 11:13–16,39–40.

AN ACTION TO TAKE: How do you reconcile the troubles you encounter in life with God's gospel of grace? What steps can you take to reach God when suffering enters your life? Visit **edwj.org/so21-22sep**

A PRAYER TO MAKE: 'Lord, "I need Thee, oh, I need Thee; Ev'ry hour I need Thee; Oh, bless me now, my Savior, I come to Thee"'. Amen.'

'https://hymnary.org/text/i_need_thee_every_hour_most_gracious_lor [accessed 15/05/2021]

Whisper of Truth

Ecclesiastes 9:9–18
'The quiet words of the wise are more to be heeded than the shouts of a ruler of fools.

Wisdom is better than weapons of war, but one sinner destroys much good.' (vv17–18)

It is interesting to note that God speaks as the still, small voice (1 Kings 19:12–13). Too often, it is the noisy soundtrack that accompanies so much of life that provokes our instinctive responses. God invites us to pause and discern God's voice, wisdom itself.

As with all music, it takes a trained ear to distinguish individual instruments. We are invited by God's Spirit to tune into God's refrain that continuously plays as part of life's symphony.

All too often we're captivated with the dramatic entrances, or the grand gesture. Yet, we cannot discover God's will and way within the cacophony of sound that overwhelms our senses; rather, it's in God's revelation alone that we can find hope and draw confidence (Isa. 30:15).

One reason we pause daily and read Scripture is that its pages alone contain God's revelation, something previously undisclosed that may surprise us. Revelation challenges our assumptions and carries us beyond our comfort zone. Whilst testing our resolve, it can only ever bring us closer to God, where we discover the true purpose of our life.

In a complex world, our hope is only ever in God. Faithfulness may not be much in fashion, but God's kingdom is established upon the faithful lives of His disciples. Each of us can quietly invest in ensuring God's purpose is realised through our life in His world.

RELATED SCRIPTURE TO CONSIDER: 1 Sam. 2; Psa. 119:105–112; 1 Cor. 1:18–31; Eph. 4:14–24.

AN ACTION TO TAKE: How might you press pause, step back from life's soundtrack and discover God's refrain for your own life? What is God revealing to you today through Scripture?

A PRAYER TO MAKE: 'Lord, open my eyes so that I might behold wonderful things throughout Your Word. Amen.' (see Psa. 119:18)

Ecclesiastes 11:7–10
'So then, banish anxiety from your heart and cast off the troubles of your body, for youth and vigour are meaningless.' (v10)

Jesus tells us to live in the moment (Matt. 6:34). Learning to do so is a skill that takes time to develop. Too often we can miss the present moment because we're consumed with past regrets or future worries. Many of us experience anxiety, the worst part of which is our inability to shift it from dominating our waking hours. It can consume our very existence, and can require professional support so that it doesn't destroy us.

The simple way Jesus approached life is something we can aspire to. There is little we can do to reverse past experience. We are forced to face today in the light of our past experiences. These can act as a drag anchor on the progress of the life we anticipated. But they don't need to rob us of encountering hope in the reality of our present, and indeed an as yet unrealised future.

A life without problems is a Hollywood fantasy. There's a shortage of princes and super heroes. Yet, we can discover that God has placed within us, through the Spirit, all the resources we require to become the super hero of our own narrative, the champion to both family, friends and neighbours.

A rich and fulfilled life owes little to natural advantage, and everything to the promise of God and our willingness and ability to lay hold of this in the present reality of every moment we encounter.

RELATED SCRIPTURE TO CONSIDER: Gen. 22:1–19; Isa. 43:16–21; Phil. 3:7–14; 2 Tim. 1:6–14.

AN ACTION TO TAKE: How do you react when you don't know precisely what is happening, or exactly where it is all going? Can you find the possibilities and challenges offered by the present moment, and then embrace them with courage, faith and hope.˙

A PRAYER TO MAKE: 'Lord, help me to trust in this moment that You are present with me and that I will see Your goodness. Amen.'

˙Adapted from Thomas Merton, '*Conjectures of a Guilty Bystander*' (London: Penguin, 1968).

Ecclesiastes 12:9–12

'Be warned, my son, of anything in addition to them. Of making many books there is no end, and much study wearies the body.' (v12)

Knowledge represents all the acts, information and skills acquired through education and experience. It is our theoretical and practical understanding of something. Scripture teaches us that our great teacher is God. The Bible provides the source for knowledge of ourselves and how we can live full and complete lives on earth (John 10:10).

Michael W Smith sings, 'Even the Darkness Is Light to You'.* This sounds contradictory, but even when we cannot see our way forward, God's Word is a lamp to our feet (Psa.119:105). This is because Scripture is God's revelation, something God makes known that offers hope and encouragement, fit for the circumstances in which we find ourselves.

In an age in which we pursue global answers to specific personal issues, we discover that one quality of the uniqueness of our mortality is that there can be no 'one size fits all' solution to life's challenges. Each one of us is born to a unique journey. God has promised to resource us for our mortal pilgrimage, yet we often feel completely unprepared for our life experiences.

It can prove problematic, and a struggle, to discern God's revelation as we enter inner turmoil or external storms. Such revelation is not readily accessible, but is the fruit of hard fought battles with ourselves and the God we have chosen to follow.

RELATED SCRIPTURE TO CONSIDER: Psa. 139; Zeph. 3:8–20; Matt 7:7–14; 1 Pet. 2:1–10.

AN ACTION TO TAKE: How confident do you feel about finding the answers to life's challenges within God's revelation through Scripture?

A PRAYER TO MAKE: 'Lord, may I find Your light in my deepest struggles and trust that You will lead me on through my life. Amen.'

*Light to You by Michael W Smith, from the album, Surrounded (Rockdown Records © 2018).

Ecclesiastes 12:13–14

'Now all has been heard; here is the conclusion of the matter: fear God and keep his commandments, for this is the duty of all mankind.' (v13)

O ur time in this world is short lived and our activities impermanent. Ecclesiastes' message is first to reflect and then to set some good priorities. In our striving for success, we may waste an opportunity to deepen our appreciation of God, who alone is eternal.

We can spend much time seeking right from wrong, yet only God knows where, and how, to draw that line. Our time is best spent seeking to live by God's wisdom. This itself often contradicts worldly wisdom and requires us to live trusting in His unrealised promises (Heb. 11:13).

The foundation for a faith-filled life is to 'fear God and keep his commandments'. Indeed, this is the prescription for fullness of life for all of humanity. But we appear wired to look into our future. Ecclesiastes teaches us that we can only navigate the present with any confidence. As we age, our thoughts may turn to legacy. Here too we are reminded that an uncertain future, subject to frequent, and abrupt, change (who predicted the pandemic and its impact?), means it is folly to plan for a future we shall never see.

Whilst life is uncertain, and often upsetting, Ecclesiastes reminds us of our frail mortality. We do well to heed this, itself a source for greater humility. We are then to pray, work and contemplate God's Word and in this way faithfully follow Jesus' teaching to nourish faith, hope and love in our own life and as a witness to others.

RELATED SCRIPTURE TO CONSIDER: Job 7:1–10; Isa. 40:6–11; 1 Cor. 3:18–23; James 4:14–17.

AN ACTION TO TAKE: In what ways might fearing God and keeping His commandments encourage you in everyday life?

A PRAYER TO MAKE: 'Lord, help me to grow content with living in the present. May I live by Your Word every day. Amen.'

Leviticus 23:33–36
'Say to the Israelites: "On the fifteenth day of the seventh month the LORD's Festival of Tabernacles begins, and it lasts for seven days."' (v34)

Traditionally, the end of September is a season of celebration in the UK. Known as Harvest Festival, it's a season of thanksgiving for the successful crop harvest. In a rural economy, harvests guaranteed feed for livestock through the winter, as well as provision of seed for the following spring's planting.

Today, we've moved from a rural to a knowledge based, technological economy. With that, we have lost touch with the land that provides so much of the daily bread we depend on.

Sukkot is the Feast of Tabernacles. Instituted by God, it invited the Jews to reflect upon God's provision over 40 years in the wilderness, and lasted seven days. The popular name for Sukkot is Festival of Joy in acknowledgement of God's sustenance as His people journeyed from Egypt to the Promised Land.

Whilst we may not have a rural existence, we can still rejoice in the fact that God remains our refuge and strength (Psa. 46:1). The tradition of offering a prayer, or saying grace, before a meal stems from this desire to recognise God as our provider, Jehovah Jireh (Gen. 22:14).

In a secular age, we have an opportunity to recover many of the traditions we discover in the Bible. They are easy to communicate to family, friends and neighbours, and establish occasions in which we simply give thanks to God for providing us with our daily bread, something we request in the Lord's Prayer (Matt. 6:11).

RELATED SCRIPTURE TO CONSIDER: Lev. 23:39–43; Neh. 8:9–18; John 7:37–44; 1 Cor. 5:6–8.

AN ACTION TO TAKE: Why not organise an evening to give thanks to God for His provision over this past year? Why not invite some friends?

A PRAYER TO MAKE: 'Lord, thank You for providing me with what I need day by day. Amen.'

Psalm 67

'The land yields its harvest; God, our God, blesses us. May God bless us still, so that all the ends of the earth will fear him.' (vv6–7)

We are familiar with annual seasons. Writing *EDWJ*, I'm focused on nature's rhythm here in the UK. Yet, wonderful news, *EDWJ* is read around the globe and so my winter is someone else's summer.

Yet, one thing we never question in the UK is that, despite complaints over delay, spring will give rise to summer. Each season will naturally follow on – year in, year out.

One way I have found useful in approaching God is to recognise that life runs through seasons. There are times of great provision and equally times of unrelenting scarcity. Yet, here I am still standing, still praying, still giving thanks, seven decades into my journey towards eternity.

God can be relied on. We may not like the season we find ourselves in, yet, like all seasons, it will pass. I used to grow depressed when the clocks went back and daylight was reduced. Now it's OK, since I have found a way to adopt a positive approach to shorter days and longer nights. After all, God can only ever lighten our darkness.

The lesson for each one of us is that we can be constrained by our darkest fears, or we can acknowledge them for what they are – anxiety – and quietly choose to place our hand in God's and wait for the arrival of His next season. Reason being; God is faithful.

RELATED SCRIPTURE TO CONSIDER: Deut. 8:7–18; Psa. 104:1–9; Luke 12:16–34; 2 Cor. 9:6–15.

AN ACTION TO TAKE: We face many different challenges in life. Waverley Abbey publishes the Insights series to help address these. Take a look by visiting **edwj.org/so21-28sep**

A PRAYER TO MAKE: 'Lord, help me, whatever the season, to trust and follow You, no matter how I feel. Amen.'

Don't Give Up

Galatians 6:7–10
'Let us not become weary in doing good, for at the proper time we will reap a harvest if we do not give up.' (v9)

There are certain unchanging laws in nature. Seeds, once planted, will germinate and produce the fruit that was embedded within them. In the same way, there are unchanging laws that underpin the ways of God. We can push against them, yet eventually the principle of that law will assert itself and we shall experience its consequences.

A brief observation of the world in which we live challenges many of the basic moral lessons we were taught as children. Wrongdoing goes unpunished and individuals benefit unjustly at the expense of others. Jesus Himself experienced the abuse of law when He was found guilty and summarily executed on Calvary. Yet He remained silent and submitted to the court's verdict. Hollywood outcomes are no less of a fantasy than the stories they breathe life into.

It's easy in the moral confusion of our world to find a rational defence for actions that we know within are unacceptable and whose consequences can negatively impact others. So, God's unchanging law is simple; live by the revelation of God's Word regardless of the consequences. This will prove tiring, for often no one may notice. Yet, our judge, God, always observes and notes our decisions and our actions.

A harvest cannot be reaped the day the seed is sown. It is only revealed after it has been buried in the ground and experienced the varying weather of the seasons. Yet, the harvest remains the only evidence of the quality and consistency of the seed.

RELATED SCRIPTURE TO CONSIDER: 1 Sam. 24; 1 Kings 21:1–19; Matt. 13:31–35; 17:14–21.

AN ACTION TO TAKE: Obeying God won't get us noticed or be rewarded but it sows the kingdom seed through our lives. Are you a kingdom farmer?

A PRAYER TO MAKE: 'Lord, help me to accept, understand and live by Your unchanging laws. Amen.'

James 3:13–18

'But the wisdom that comes from heaven is first of all pure; then peace-loving, considerate, submissive, full of mercy and good fruit, impartial and sincere.' (v17)

Behaviour originates within each of us. Knowing how we're expected to behave, and then behaving in that way, is never guaranteed. It depends on what we allow to initiate our behaviour.

Looking back, I can recall behaviour where I've disappointed myself. When I'm the centre of my world, then my behaviour is selfish. If I'm fearful, I may fail in my responsibility to love my neighbour.

One great battle we have in deepening our friendship with God is in living lives that reveal God's faith, hope and love. Previous mistakes are easily confessed, forgiven and forgotten. Yet, when that forgetfulness extends to my present and future behaviour, I'm in danger of creating a cycle of behaviours that are as damaging to me as they are to others.

The apostles, writing to the early church, were at pains to point out that choosing God was to embrace a lifestyle often at odds with contemporary standards of behaviour. The New Testament offers us instruction both on what God requires and how such requirements are realised through prayer and obedience.

The letters were sent to the Church; for we are accountable to God most effectively when we are mutually accountable, or known, to each other. A word of encouragement, or a gentle rebuke, have been the tools I've needed to help me nurture my walk with God. It's how we each learn to live every day with Jesus.

RELATED SCRIPTURE TO CONSIDER: 1 Chron. 29:10–19; Jer. 7:1–15; Phil. 1:27–30; Col. 3:1–17.

AN ACTION TO TAKE: Take time at the end of the day, or each week, to reflect on your behaviour. Does it reflect the best of God, or are there areas that would benefit from some attention?

A PRAYER TO MAKE: 'Lord, help me to draw on God's wisdom and live as He intends. Amen.'

Hebrews 12:11–13
'No discipline seems pleasant at the time, but painful. Later on, however, it produces a harvest of righteousness and peace for those who have been trained by it.' (v11)

We are accustomed to the concept of training. From sports to artistic accomplishment, our ability benefits from consistent training; learning specific skills to succeed in a certain activity. No surprise that the same is true in achieving a righteous life.

Righteousness simply means that our words and actions mirror each other. One of the greatest criticisms the Church has faced over the years is one of hypocrisy; too many instances where words and actions don't match.

The best defence we can mount is not to engage in a war of words. Rather, to redouble our efforts to live consistently, where our thoughts and actions match the belief we proclaim and the truth Scripture reveals.

Each one of us knows where the blurred edges exist in our own witness to Christ. Our best response is to go in search of a training programme that will strengthen our performance and so complete the race God has set before us (Heb. 12:1–2).

You can find useful free resources on the Waverley Abbey website. Also, a spiritual life audit that you can complete. Our whole ministry is directed to supporting everyone to live every day with Jesus. So make it your ambition not only to participate in the race of life representing God, but to complete it in serving Jesus' kingdom cause of loving God and serving others.

RELATED SCRIPTURE TO CONSIDER: 1 Sam. 17:32–51; 1 Chron. 6:31–32; 1 Tim. 6:6–16; Heb. 12:18–29.

AN ACTION TO TAKE: Consider buying *Strengthen Your Core. Practical Spiritual Formation for Every Day* by Jenny Campbell from waverleyabbeyresources. org edwj.org/so21-1oct

A PRAYER TO MAKE: 'Lord, strengthen my resolve to train in Your service and complete the race of life by faithfully serving You. Amen.'

Malachi 3:6–12

'Bring the whole tithe into the storehouse, that there may be food in my house. Test me in this,' says the LORD Almighty, 'and see if I will not throw open the floodgates of heaven and pour out so much blessing that there will not be room enough to store it.' (v10)

Disobedience is more often a result of neglect than deliberate intention. Life is all consuming, with many legitimate demands on our time and energy. Our heart is for God, but we're simply overwhelmed.

The good news is that God is consistent, and invites us, whenever we can, to make our approach. The little we invest will return to us a harvest that not only satisfies our own needs but replenishes our energy so that we have sufficient to support and encourage others.

One reason I break my day up with short times of prayer is to remind myself that without God I can only fail myself, my family and friends. These breaks are no longer than a few minutes. I have a set series of prayers that I repeat. This is my refreshment; a reminder that without God I can do nothing (John 15:5).

As we take time for replenishment, much like our refreshment and meal breaks, we renew our spiritual strength and refocus on the one whom we serve, the source of all life. Consequently, we are reminded of the blessing that is ours daily in Christ Jesus.

If we regularly carry our thanks to God, we shall replenish a storehouse from which we can draw encouragement and hope in difficult times. Failure to do so may mean that, at the point of our greatest need, we might have no resources to draw on.

RELATED SCRIPTURE TO CONSIDER: Lev. 26:1–13; Psa. 34:8–14; Joel 1:11–20; 1 Pet. 3:8–12.

AN ACTION TO TAKE: Consider how you can create touch points with God throughout your day, and store up blessings by offering thanks to God regularly.

A PRAYER TO MAKE: 'Lord, I enthusiastically praise You at all times; Your praise will always be on my lips as I will continually glory in the Lord; let the afflicted hear and rejoice. Amen.' (based on Psa. 34:1–2)

Be Healed

James 5:13–16

'Therefore confess your sins to each other and pray for each other so that you may be healed. The prayer of a righteous person is powerful and effective.' (v16)

L earning to live with an open heart before God and others is always a challenge. We are instinctively suspicious of other people. We easily feel vulnerable about sharing honestly our feelings and experiences.

There is some wisdom here, for being open with complete strangers is never a good idea. This is why God invites us into a shared meeting space with other like-minded people. Together we learn the character and nature of our God. We discover how it is we can grow in faith and practice in serving God. The benefits of a small group cannot be overstated. Here I can build trustworthy relationships built on knowledge and trust.

Within our heart there is the desire to be known for who we are. This is the search that drives many in seeking a companion to share their life with. In small groups we can learn from the experience of others, across a wide age group. We can also find the courage and confidence to share our own fears and failings.

Until I am ready to be known for who I really am, I am limited in the extent to which I can pray in integrity for the needs of others (Prov. 28:26). Once I am known for who I am, I begin to live with an authenticity that speaks of my confidence in God. Once my confidence is in God, then anxiety falls away for I have made my home with the Lord of life.

RELATED SCRIPTURE TO CONSIDER: Prov. 12:13–28; Matt. 16:21–28; John 15:9–27; 1 Pet. 4:7–11.

AN ACTION TO TAKE: Are you part of a small group where you can build confidence in God together to trust each other with who you truly are? Are you willing to be known completely?

A PRAYER TO MAKE: 'Lord, help me to share my life with others so that there is a harvest of love in our Christian life and witness together. Amen.'

John 6:32–40

'Then Jesus declared, "I am the bread of life. Whoever comes to me will never go hungry, and whoever believes in me will never be thirsty."' (v35)

Over the next few days we'll look at Jesus' eight 'I am' statements. These provide specific indicators to Jesus' unique qualities. They reveal Jesus as God's Son and not simply a good teacher.

Our mortal lives are fuelled by the food we eat. We know some foods are 'healthy' whilst others are regarded as 'junk'. The difference? Healthy food offers 'our bodies the nutrients they need to run efficiently and fight off sickness and disease'.* Junk food, usually processed, threatens 'empty calories—foods... full of fat and sugar', lacking the many nutrients that help the body focus, exercise, or perform'.**

The source of our God encounter is as important to spiritual health as the source of our food is to our body. We're invited, by Jesus Himself, to draw our life from Him. How? Through Scripture, itself God's Word. It transforms our understanding of God, ourselves, others, and the world in which we live.

God's Word meets our inner hunger not our natural appetite, which the people followed Jesus for after the feeding of the five thousand (John 6:26–27), rather than because of a deep yearning for inner peace and understanding. Once found, there's nothing that can compare, and all other ambitions fade. Every appetite we have ever experienced can be satisfied from God's larder this is the challenge that greets every Christian, one we pursue daily.

RELATED SCRIPTURE TO CONSIDER: 2 Sam. 22:31–37; Ezek. 37:3–14; John 1:1–18; 1 Thess. 2:13–16.

AN ACTION TO TAKE: If you are battling with something that robs you of God's supply then it may help to speak with someone. At Waverley Abbey we can support you in finding someone to speak with. Visit edwj.org/so21-4oct

A PRAYER TO MAKE: 'Lord, I approach You as the bread that satisfies my deepest hunger. Help me in my struggles so that I am wholly satisfied with the bread of life. Amen.'

*independence.edu/blog/junk-food-vs-health-food [accessed 18/05/2021]
**Ibid.

John 8:12

'When Jesus spoke again to the people, he said, "I am the light of the world. Whoever follows me will never walk in darkness, but will have the light of life."' (v12)

Throughout Scripture, God is associated with light: the burning bush at Moses' call (Exod. 3:3–4), the pillar of fire in the wilderness (Exod. 13:21). The psalmist spoke of God as light (Psa. 27:1), whilst the prophet promised, 'The LORD shall be your everlasting light' (Isa. 60:19) and spoke of the Messiah as light (Isa. 60:1). As a child, Simeon hailed Jesus as 'a light to reveal God to the nations' (Luke 2:32 NLT).˙

Light drives away our fears in the dead of night. It reveals things for what they truly are. It is the source of all life and we are reliant upon it, for our health, mental wellbeing and food.

So Jesus couldn't have chosen a more critical element to illustrate how God is essential for our total welfare. When we are uncertain, we can seek God as a light source to show us the way forward. Like Moses, we may shrink back from God's guiding light (Exod. 4:13), yet if we follow, albeit hesitantly, God will bring us into a greater appreciation of His love, even if we request some additional support (Exod. 4:15).

When I get lost through my own wilfulness or blinded by life experience, I can call out to the light of the world and recover my bearings. Obviously I may only see a few feet in front of me, but that's sufficient light to enable me to walk in the right direction. I can also have confidence that this is a light whose batteries never fail.

RELATED SCRIPTURE TO CONSIDER: Gen. 1:1–5; Dan. 2:19–23; Matt. 5:14–16; James 1:12–18.

AN ACTION TO TAKE: Are there dark shadows where you need to invite God to shine His light and guide your way?

A PRAYER TO MAKE: 'Lord, light up my life and turn my darkness into day. Amen.' (Psa. 18:28)

˙See also: loyolapress.com/catholic-resources/scripture-and-tradition/jesus-and-the-new-testament/who-do-you-say-that-i-am-names-for-jesus/jesus-the-light-of-the-world/

John 10:7–13
**'I am the gate; whoever enters through me will be saved.
They will come in and go out, and find pasture. The thief
comes only to steal and kill and destroy; I have come that
they may have life, and have it to the full.'** (vv9–10)

A gate serves a purpose. It keeps things out, or in. So we enter our homes and close the door to keep unwanted strangers from entering uninvited. Yet, a prisoner is locked inside a cell to keep them from going out.

Similarly, we have the opportunity to invite Jesus to be the gate to protect us from damage arising from influences and impulses that work to destroy us, albeit slowly rather than all at once. I remember, whilst caring for my first wife, how I found myself drinking too much for my liking. I was drawing comfort from a source other than God. This was not done maliciously, but simply under the stress of the demands that caring places on the carer. Making my way to the bottle bank, I recognised I may well be becoming dependent upon alcohol. With God's insight and help I shut the door, because it was not what I wanted.

Again, it's easy to hold certain emotions within, whilst presenting a well-ordered persona to a watching world. However, such internal self-control can eventually cause us to break under the strain. We have tried to lock something deep inside that actually needs to be acknowledged and released.

God provides us with the gate that helps us to establish the normal Christian life revealed through Scripture. We must remain vigilant, for there are always those seeking to take advantage when we fail to shut the door behind us.

RELATED SCRIPTURE TO CONSIDER: 2 Chron. 23:12–21; Psa. 84; Matt. 7:13–23; Rev. 3:14–22.

AN ACTION TO TAKE: What steps can you take to ensure that God is the gatekeeper of your life?

A PRAYER TO MAKE: 'Lord, may I work to always maintain You as the gatekeeper of my life, and so resist the thieves who wish to steal from me. Amen.'

The Shepherd

John 10:11–21

'I am the good shepherd. The good shepherd lays down his life for the sheep. The hired hand is not the shepherd and does not own the sheep. So when he sees the wolf coming, he abandons the sheep and runs away. Then the wolf attacks the flock and scatters it.' (vv11–12)

Jesus identifies Himself as a shepherd. His responsibility is to care for His flock, and humanity is that flock. The skill of every shepherd is to ensure sufficient grazing for the whole flock, from the youngest to the oldest. There is no discrimination based on age.

Whilst the flock travels as a group, the shepherd must be vigilant to identify any individual sheep who may be struggling through injury or illness. In like manner, God cares for us as His family as well as for each one of us individually.

Living in the open, travelling many miles in seeking nourishment, the flock is at risk night and day. With no natural defence save from crowding together, every sheep relies upon the shepherd for their protection. Being vulnerable, and tasty, there is no shortage of predators who wait for an opportunity to steal away a member of the flock.

This appears to be such a simple message and it is. For we, the sheep who have gone astray, are gathered together by the great shepherd, Jesus Himself (Psa. 79:13). He walks with us as we pursue our lives, wandering wherever we choose. When we find ourselves isolated and lonely, fighting our personal battles, the good shepherd will find us, retrieve us and restore us to the flock where we belong.

RELATED SCRIPTURE TO CONSIDER: Isa. 53; Psa. 100; 119:169–176; Matt. 25:31–46.

AN ACTION TO TAKE: Invite Jesus, the great shepherd of the sheep (Heb. 13:20–21), to keep you in the flock of His choosing and respond to His gentle leading in good times and bad.

A PRAYER TO MAKE: 'Lord, 'I trust You to show me the way I pray, dear Lord, don't let me stray. Help me to see my path You chose." Amen.'

˚healingpresenceministry.com/rhonda-milner/the-prayer-of-the-wandering-sheep [accessed 20/05/2021]

John 11:17–44

'Jesus said to her, "I am the resurrection and the life. The one who believes in me will live, even though they die; and whoever lives by believing in me will never die. Do you believe this?"' (vv25–26)

We must each personally face and address our death, an unavoidable consequence of life. Jesus invites us to place confidence in His promise of life beyond the grave.

Thomas à Kempis (1380–1471) wrote, 'If you have ever seen a man die, remember that you, too, must go the same way. In the morning consider that you may not live till evening, and when evening comes do not dare to promise yourself the dawn. Be always ready, therefore, and so live that death will never take you unprepared.'*

Jesus demonstrates that He is the resurrection and life. Lazarus, dead for four days, is restored to life by Jesus. He cannot resist Jesus' command, 'Lazarus, come out!' (v43). He had to name Lazarus, or every corpse in that communal tomb would have been resuscitated, for Jesus is the resurrection and the life forever. Death itself is subject to Jesus.

Lazarus, like all those Jesus healed, remained mortal and, as such, faced death again. However, the promise was illustrated in plain sight that life is found in Christ alone. What we fear we have lost can be revived by the life and love of Jesus. It's a sign of the power He has over every expression of death. This means the anticipated fruit from missed opportunities and the opportunity for recovery from unexpected experiences. Jesus finds us in our darkest night and leads us into a new day (vv9–10).

One reason we live every day with Jesus is to discover life where we feared, and found, only death whilst stumbling in the dark. Jesus offers everyone a fresh dawn.

RELATED SCRIPTURE TO CONSIDER: 2 Sam. 12:1–14; 1 Kings 17:7–24; Luke 19:1–9; John 4:7–30.

AN ACTION TO TAKE: What dreams will you invite God to resuscitate?

A PRAYER TO MAKE: 'Lord, in my darkest night may I look towards the light of Your love. Amen.'

*Thomas à Kempis, *The Imitation of Christ* (London: Penguin, 2005), Book I, chap. 23.

John 14:1–6

'Jesus answered, "I am the way and the truth and the life. No one comes to the Father except through me. If you really know me, you will know my Father as well. From now on, you do know him and have seen him."' (vv6–7)

Thomas asked a great question, 'Lord, we don't know where you are going, so how can we know the way?' Throughout history, humanity has tried to control its future. A recent article described church leaders as looking for post-pandemic confidence 'in data and prediction'.* The future will always remain uncertain; only by following Jesus in faith can we find our way.

Life offers us many 'ways' to live. However, most of us are looking for a way that is true; one that is trustworthy, enriching our life without disappointing us. Where we may become the best expression of ourselves, and invest in the encouragement and wellbeing of others.

A way of life offers a pattern of behaviour. Scripture reveals how God has made us and how we can maximise our life experience. There are frameworks and rules; for we know a game of soccer is ruined if players ignore the referee's whistle or the pitch's limitations.

Rules exist to improve our quality of life. They help us to work with others in a creative social environment. In choosing to follow Jesus' way, I live the life I was designed for one reason why engaging with the Bible daily is essential. We cannot know where we are going without consulting God, our guide. It's the reason Waverley Abbey Trust wants to ensure everyone enjoys access to *Every Day with Jesus*. Give a copy to someone you know and care for.

RELATED SCRIPTURE TO CONSIDER: Gen. 6:9–22; Isa. 30:15–26; Acts 9:1–19; 2 Cor. 5:1–10.

AN ACTION TO TAKE: Have you chosen God's way of life? What are the challenges in entrusting your future into God's hands?

A PRAYER TO MAKE: 'Lord, teach me through Scripture how I might live and serve You and live a fulfilling life. Amen.'

*Alan Roxburgh and Martin Robinson, 'Proper Confidence: Being God's People in a New Era' (*JMP*, Spring 2021) journalofmissionalpractice.com/proper-confidence/ [accessed 22/05/2021]

John 15:1–17

"I am the true vine, and my Father is the gardener. He cuts off every branch in me that bears no fruit, while every branch that does bear fruit he prunes so that it will be even more fruitful.' (vv1–2)

Gardening is not everyone's cup of tea. Jesus reminds us what every gardener knows; prune hard and the yield is greatly increased.

Once we have made our peace with God, we face the challenge of staying close to Him. Not because of some great sin, but through the disregard that familiarity can bring. Who hasn't struggled with our Christian walk that's become little more than a habit?

All relationships can wither if we fail to nurture them. We may know God's truth, yet lose our first love (Rev. 2:4), and therefore sight, of God. Every relationship needs habits and practices to facilitate daily demands. But be alert! Don't let the romance die.

Patterns of behaviour ensure life's mundane tasks are fulfilled. However, never lose sight of the fact that relationships are not simply to navigate life's many demands. They are to encourage us to unlock the best within each other, to grow in affection, understanding and appreciation. We can only do this by seeking to enable someone else to become the best expression of themself. This is how God approaches each one of us; He has our best interests at heart.

Of course, in Jesus we can expect no improvement, for He is the fullness of God. Yet, we can discover that His commitment is always to help us become the very best version of ourselves. Abiding in Christ is keeping our first love alive, so that in every mundane activity we find joy in doing it for, and out of love of, God.

RELATED SCRIPTURE TO CONSIDER: Exod. 34:1–9; Psa. 103; Heb. 3:1–14; James 4:7–12.

AN ACTION TO TAKE: What steps will you take to keep your friendship with God fresh and alive?

A PRAYER TO MAKE: 'Lord, may I never become so familiar with You that I lose my first love. Amen.'

Nehemiah 9:5–6

'You alone are the LORD. You made the heavens, even the highest heavens, and all their starry host, the earth and all that is on it, the seas and all that is in them. You give life to everything, and the multitudes of heaven worship you.' (v6)

Considering the reasons we have to praise and thank God, we do well to pause and consider our life's source. The Bible says that God formed humanity and breathed life into His creation (Gen. 2:7). The word for 'breath' also means 'spirit' and refers to the life of God that inhabits every believer in the Holy Spirit (1 Cor. 6:19).

It's easy to take life for granted and then a global pandemic stops us in our tracks. Familiarity ends in a moment and we realise we are part of something far greater than ourselves, with no power to manage our environment.

As disciples, we are part of the total creation of our heavenly Father. There is nothing that lies outside of God's control. We confidently give thanks to our God for creating and sustaining our world. It will continue until God chooses to conclude time as we know it, signalled with the return of the risen Christ (1 Thess. 4:16).

We can live life one of two ways. Physically, living and working whilst bound by the limitations of our mortality. Or, through the salvation of God, being continually transformed by God's Spirit and growing into who God originally created us to become. We need not be shackled to the limitations of our mortal and rational self, but are invited to see ourselves as part of a boundless, infinite plan. So we give joyful thanks to God, creator of all.

RELATED SCRIPTURE TO CONSIDER: Neh. 9:7–37; Psa. 8; Eph. 2; 1 Thess. 4:13–5:11.

AN ACTION TO TAKE: Consider what difference it makes to your view of yourself, others and the world in which you live knowing you have eternity in your heart.

A PRAYER TO MAKE: 'Lord, I pause to praise and celebrate that You are the creator and Lord of all creation. Amen.'

Write to **micha@edwj.org** and I'll write back personally and in confidence as soon as I can.

1 Chronicles 29:10–13

**'Yours, LORD, is the greatness and the power and the
glory and the majesty and the splendour, for everything
in heaven and earth is yours. Yours, LORD, is the
kingdom; you are exalted as head over all.'** (v11)

It is impossible to exhaust language that describes God's character
and qualities. I find myself speechless as I meditate upon the Lord.
Not simply a lord but the Lord of Lords. In other words, there is no
power or authority that exceeds that of our God.

It's remarkable that one so self-sufficient would want to take time
with us. In our celebrity culture, our access to the stars is usually
limited to the pages of glossy magazines or social media snippets. The
greatest celebrity of all time, in fact the one who created time itself,
chooses to hang out with those of us who are dependent upon Him for
our very existence.

I remind myself that I am not to rush into God's presence, forgetting
the privilege I enjoy at God's invitation. When accepting any invitation,
we usually take steps to find a suitable gift for our host and give them
our full attention. Distraction is regarded as rude disinterest.

We enjoy an open invitation to spend time with God; how can we
resist this opportunity to converse with the Lord of Lords? It is in such
moments that we learn more of our God who we've chosen to serve.
Indeed, as with every relationship, it's the only way we can strengthen
our friendship (Heb. 4:14–16).

Failure to take such time with God will lead to a loss of conviction
and create distance between us and God, a distance for which we
alone are responsible.

RELATED SCRIPTURE TO CONSIDER: Deut. 10:12–22; Isa. 45:5–8; Acts 10:34–44;
Rev. 19:9–16.

AN ACTION TO TAKE: How do you prepare when accepting God's personal
invitation to spend time with Him?

A PRAYER TO MAKE: 'Lord, I thank You that I am known and always welcomed by
the Lord of Lords. Amen.'

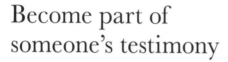

Become part of someone's testimony

Our Bible reading notes are read by hundreds of thousands of people around the world, and *Every Day with Jesus* and *Inspiring Women Every Day* have recently been made free in the UK. We want everyone, whatever their financial means, to have access to these resources that help them walk each day with our Saviour.

Here's what one Every Day with Jesus reader wrote to us:

Ever since I started using Everyday with Jesus, I reconnected to the Lord directly again. It deals with my day to day and minute to minute problems in details. Guiding me in the most solemn and right direction for a dedicated Christian living.

As we trust in God's provision, we know there are costs to providing this ministry. Do you have a passion for God's Word changing lives? Could supporting this vision be a way in which you serve?

A gift of just £2 a month from you will put daily Bible reading notes into the hands of at least one person who is hungry to know God and experience His presence every day.

Visit **waverleyabbeyresources.org/donate** to become part of someone's testimony, or use the form at the back of these notes.

Isaiah 9:2–7

'And he will be called Wonderful Counsellor, Mighty God, Everlasting Father, Prince of Peace.' (v6b)

Not only are we invited to converse with the Lord of Lords, we enjoy access to the source of all wisdom. The very meaning of life is crafted through God's act of creation, redemption and return. This is the sign of a loving, caring God. One who creates us in His image (Gen. 1:27), comes, finds and rescues us in our sin (Col. 1:13–14), and will return to restore His kingdom in completeness (1 Pet. 1:3–5).

It is self-evident that contemporary life whilst offering so many benefits also makes demands on us. Counsellors have never been so busy and the UK national narrative revolves around the fragile state of our mental health. Although as a nation we have never been richer, or enjoyed more leisure time owing to the multiplicity of technological answers to meet the demands of daily living, we appear to be no closer to contentment.

Jesus is Himself prophesied as the 'Prince of Peace', the source of all contentment. In my own life I have experienced the good, the bad and the ugly; yet although often struggling to hang onto God in life's realities, I've fought my way through to accepting and clinging to the truth found within God's Word. Anxiety remains a constant companion, yet it is far more domesticated and subject to God's peace once I turn back to God and rest in His promises. A discipline always, yet one that produces a harvest of rest.

RELATED SCRIPTURE TO CONSIDER: Num. 6:22–27; Psa. 4; John 16:16–33; Phil 4:4–9.

AN ACTION TO TAKE: It's important to take care of our mental health. Waverley Abbey publishes the Insights series that cover many important topics: see them at **edwj.org/so21-13oct**

A PRAYER TO MAKE: 'Lord, in peace I will rest, for You alone make me dwell in safety. Amen.' (Psa. 4:8)

1 John 4:13–21

'And so we know and rely on the love God has for us. God is love. Whoever lives in love lives in God, and God in them.' (v16)

We recognise that a fundamental human need is our desire to be loved. Yet, today there are more stories of failed love and fractured families than at any time in history. Despite this evidence, individuals still risk everything in their search for love.

Love has been described as, 'a set of emotions and behaviors characterized by intimacy, passion, and commitment'.* In searching for an example of love, we could not find a better expression than that of Jesus. Jesus was moved to tears at the grave of His friend Lazarus (John 11:33–35). He was emotionally invested in His mission and with the people He came to serve. Jesus' behaviour was characterised by grace (John 1:14). He was passionate and deeply committed to His mission of salvation (Mark 1:1415 . He demonstrated the qualities that prove the reality of a love that lasts and offers resilience in the face of life's demands. In response, we are invited to consider our behaviours and the thought patterns driving them.

Has our relationship with God moved beyond an intellectual understanding to an intimate love relationship with our Lord (John 12:3)? Such an intimacy produces a passion for God and His work. We are able to direct our energies to serving God, living by God's Word and letting go of our preferences that often conflict with God's purpose.

RELATED SCRIPTURE TO CONSIDER: Psa. 136; Hos. 14; 1 Cor. 13; 1 John 2:1–11.

AN ACTION TO TAKE: Love is tough to find, perhaps tougher to sustain. What does love look like in your life and experience?

A PRAYER TO MAKE: 'Lord, may I learn to practise a love that is patient, kind, contented and humble. Amen.' (1 Cor. 13:4)

*verywellmind.com/what-is-love-2795343 [accessed 22/05/2021]

Deuteronomy 7:7–9

'Know therefore that the LORD your God is God; he is the faithful God, keeping his covenant of love to a thousand generations of those who love him and keep his commandments.' (v9)

Faithfulness is one acid test of love. When Katey, my first wife, required the support of external care as multiple sclerosis developed, I well remember being advised by a social worker that it would be quite understandable if I couldn't cope and chose to walk away from my marriage. I told her that, whilst I had little experience of my capacity as a carer, I'd made commitments before God, family and friends at my wedding that meant I didn't enjoy the freedom to walk away.

It certainly was a rough ride. I learnt a lot about faithfulness from my many failures and few successes. Caring is not naturally rewarding; it demands grit and determination, qualities we need to go in search of. If love were no more than an emotion, faithfulness would crumble at the first obstacle.

Our model for faithfulness is found in God's willingness to stay with us, despite those seasons in life when our love is lukewarm. God is never indifferent or apathetic, qualities that often affect our personal commitments. We can falter or fail countless times, yet God will always be there to pick us up, brush us down and encourage us to return to His welcome, loving embrace. Despite voices that tell us we lie beyond God's love because of our attitudes or actions, remember God's love is always unfailing (Rom. 8:38–39).

RELATED SCRIPTURE TO CONSIDER: 1 Chron. 16:34–36; Psa. 86; Rom. 5:1–11; Gal. 2:11–21.

AN ACTION TO TAKE: Where, and to whom, do you turn when life gets tough and you lose sight of a faithful God? It's good to be prepared ahead of difficult times.

A PRAYER TO MAKE: 'Lord, it's said, "When the going gets tough, the tough get going". Help me stay with You and not walk away from You in such tough times. Amen.'

'When the Going Gets Tough, The Tough Get Going (*Jewel of the Nile* soundtrack) by Barry J. Eastmond, Billy Ocean, Robert J. Lange and Wayne Brathwaite (Zomba Enterprises; Aqua Music Ltd © 1985).

Psalm 62:5–8

'Truly he is my rock and my salvation; he is my fortress, I shall not be shaken. My salvation and my honour depend on God; he is my mighty rock, my refuge.' (vv6–7)

Pilgrims making their way to Lindisfarne, or Holy Island, in Northumbria, Northern England, must cross on a path that only exists at low tide. Halfway across is a refuge, built in case a pilgrim gets caught by the swift incoming tide as they cross.

A pilgrim is a traveller, and as disciples our journey is living every day with Jesus. Life itself is a causeway subject to rising and falling tides that at times threaten to swamp us. In such times, God acts as our refuge, a tower that keeps us safe from the threat of a rising tide.

Caught on the causeway, it's a judgment call if I seek to beat the tide and make my destination, or wait it out in an uncomfortable shelter. Such a wait presents an interruption to my plans. It demands that I sit tight, often alone and with few provisions for something so unplanned.

In such moments I find time to think. I am literally alone with myself and God, with few distractions. What an opportunity to reflect, consider God, and give thanks. Life is busy and interruptions are usually one way God gets our undivided attention. Our choice lies in choosing whether we will be consumed with our frustrations or take hold of this unanticipated opportunity to seek and find God where and when we least expect to search for Him.

RELATED SCRIPTURE TO CONSIDER: Deut. 33:26–29; Ruth 2:2–13; 2 Cor. 4:7–18; 12:1–10.

AN ACTION TO TAKE: When events interrupt your plans, how do you find God within the swirl of emotions that engulf you? It is in quiet and in trust that we find our strength (Isa. 30:15).

A PRAYER TO MAKE: 'Lord, thank You that I can take refuge with You when life overwhelms me and I struggle to cope. Amen.'

2 Samuel 22:2–7
'The LORD is my rock, my fortress and my deliverer' (v2)

One thing we know is that ultimately we shall see God face to face. Whatever life serves up to us, nothing can separate us from God (Rom. 8:38–39). The process we must travel through may prove testing, yet every step of the way God's hand holds us. We may need to find courage and confidence in equal measure, but God is our strong deliverer (Psa. 140:7).

The verse today is taken from David's paean of praise at the way God delivered him from both his enemies and his own deliberate disobedience. The testimony of so many characters whose lives are recorded in Scripture gives us hope and builds our own faith. One further reason why we turn to God's Word to strengthen and deepen our walk with God.

Life unfolds day by day, and none of us knows what each fresh day will reveal, what demands it will make upon us. Our own life, and the lives of those we love, cannot predict where the future will carry us. We know God is faithful, yet our personal adventure demands courage when we meet a challenge for which we feel totally unprepared. At such a moment, our confidence in God is tested. Are we able to entrust our present into God's care?

Jesus promises to be with us to the very end of the age (Matt. 28:20). How real and effective is God's presence to me, today?

RELATED SCRIPTURE TO CONSIDER: Psa. 20; Dan. 3:16–29; Acts 16:25–34; Phil. 4:11–13.

AN ACTION TO TAKE: List some of the ways in which you have discovered God to be your deliverer.

A PRAYER TO MAKE: 'Lord, with Your help I can advance with my life whatever walls I need to climb over. Amen.' (2 Sam. 22:30)

Exodus 15:1–2
**'The LORD is my strength and my defence; he
has become my salvation.'** (v2a)

T he Israelites expressed their terror as they saw Pharaoh and the
Egyptians pursuing them (Exod. 14:10–11). They didn't organise a
praise party. A reminder that it is easier giving thanks looking back
from a place of safety than when facing an insurmountable problem.
God invites us to give thanks from a place of faith, whilst still waiting
to experience a practical solution. We must pause, believe and give
thanks to God (Exod. 14:13–14).

Learning to give thanks as an expression of our faith can seem
premature. We cannot give thanks for the details of God's provision
whilst they are still unknown. However, we can give thanks that God is
with us in the problem and remains our only hope in times of trouble
(Heb. 10:23). We give thanks for the fact that God can and will deliver us.

In reality, this is the commitment we make at salvation. We accept
that Jesus is Saviour, has risen from the grave and has the authority to
forgive our sins. As we ask for God's forgiveness and acceptance, we
are confident by faith that God will bring us into eternity. One problem;
no one but Christ has seen eternity. We will only experience the
fulfilment of the promise once we have died, and yet we give thanks to
God now for our salvation.

We are invited to give thanks before the parting of the Red Sea, and
not simply after we have safely crossed.

RELATED SCRIPTURE TO CONSIDER: Job 11:13–20; Psa. 42; Rom. 8:22–27;
Eph. 1:18–23.

AN ACTION TO TAKE: You can't know how God will answer your prayers, but you
can give thanks that God will answer you in His own time and way. Can you
give thanks for that?

A PRAYER TO MAKE: 'Lord, I thank You that my fears can be faced through the
hope I have in You. Amen.'

1 Samuel 2:1–10

'Do not keep talking so proudly or let your mouth speak such arrogance, for the LORD is a God who knows, and by him deeds are weighed.' (v3)

Nowadays, we are bombarded with words across a variety of platforms. It's increasingly difficult to hear the Word of God. Not only is God's Word drowned out in the clamour, but we easily become influenced by these many voices.

God's command is to love God and neighbour (Mark 12:30–31). All of our decisions and actions are to pass through this critical filter to inform us how to live, as we choose God's way as our primary purpose on earth. Every day we are being conformed into Jesus' image (Rom. 8:29). Our life is a process of growing into Christlike maturity (Eph. 4:11–13).

Hannah knows the agony of unanswered prayer, the sound of bragging from her rival, and the loss of self-confidence, despite the favour of her husband. Her world is defined by the voices of others and she turns to God in her misery and grief with a heartfelt prayer, itself the source of further misunderstanding and criticism.

Hannah dedicates herself to God and then her prayer is answered (1 Sam. 1:11). Too often, our prayers serve our own felt needs. God acts in our lives so that we might continue our growth in understanding and service of God. It is always good to ask ourselves why we are praying for something. Is it in my interest or God's? In reality, God's interest is always my best interest. Remember, we are invited by Jesus to pray for His kingdom to come on the earth.

RELATED SCRIPTURE TO CONSIDER: 1 Sam 1:1–17; Isa. 57:11–13; Acts 4:1–31; James 1:2–8.

AN ACTION TO TAKE: Our challenge is in discerning what God wants from what I want. Are you willing to explore this path of prayer?

A PRAYER TO MAKE: 'Lord, may Your kingdom come and Your will be done on earth as it is in heaven. Amen.' (Matt. 6:10)

Jonah 2:3–4
**'I said, "I have been banished from your sight; yet I
will look again towards your holy temple."'** (v4)

Jonah's first response was to run! Called east to Nineveh in Iraq,
he headed west towards Lebanon. Yet, God interrupted his
journey. Now inside a large fish, Jonah takes time to reflect and
respond to God.

Wherever we run in our attempts to avoid God, He always knows
where we are. We can never outrun His love. Our response always
remains ours to make, but there's never any doubt about God's desire
to befriend and lead us into the purpose for which we were created.

With some enforced leisure, Jonah, much like the Prodigal Son,
reflects on his choices and circumstances and decides to respond
to God's call. He declares, 'But I, with shouts of grateful praise, will
sacrifice to you' (v9).

It's possible to give thanks when bad things happen. God uses life
experience to grab our attention. C.S. Lewis wrote, 'God whispers to us
in our pleasures, speaks in our conscience, but shouts in our pains: it is
His megaphone to rouse a deaf world'.[*]

We may seek to avoid pain, but it's an essential part of our defence
system, and helps keep us safe. Anyone suffering from HSAN II, where
they don't experience physical pain, will confirm that.[**]

In difficult, uncomfortable even painful situations, we can choose
to give thanks as we connect once more with God and make our way
forward with a renewed sense of identity and purpose.

RELATED SCRIPTURE TO CONSIDER: Isa. 30:1–18; Jonah 1:9–2:10; Luke 15:11–32;
James 1:2–8; 4:7–10.

AN ACTION TO TAKE: When God resorts to a megaphone to talk to you, pause and
ask yourself 'why?'.

A PRAYER TO MAKE: 'Lord, thank You that You never despair of nor abandon me.
May I reflect and then return to You. Amen.' (Matt. 6:10)

[*]C.S. Lewis, *The Problem of Pain* (London: Collins, 2012), chap. 6.
[**]Michaela Haas, *Bouncing Forward. The Art and Science of Cultivating Resilience* (New York: Enliven
Books, 2015), chap. 7.

Acts 9:10–19

'Lord,' Ananias answered, 'I have heard many reports about this man and all the harm he has done to your holy people in Jerusalem. And he has come here with authority from the chief priests to arrest all who call on your name.' (vv13–14)

There are some people who may never know the extent of their part in global mission. Ananias is one of these. We have this brief mention in Scripture, but through his courage and faithfulness, God released the powerful and influential ministry of Paul.

When we ask God to speak to us, and then hear God's voice, He expects us to respond. I imagine that Ananias daily prayed to God, and one night God spoke back very precisely with details of a task, a person and an address. A word of knowledge, in fact (1 Cor. 12:8).

In his excitement, Ananias realised that God's invitation was to step into the lion's den; did he want to, as the song goes, 'Dare to be a Daniel, Dare to stand alone! Dare to have a purpose firm! Dare to make it known'?" He knew the risks and perhaps the first knocking Saul heard was that of Ananias' knees.

Obeying God always demands courage. Confronting his fears, Ananias went and released Saul through prayer and the whole world became a beneficiary of one person's obedience.

We give thanks for the miracle delivered through Ananias, and for the many miracles that take place every day because of the simple obedience of people around the globe. We can never know the full impact of our obedience, nor do we need to. God only ever asks that we are faithful with what He asks of us and that we respond, 'Yes, Lord, send me'.

RELATED SCRIPTURE TO CONSIDER: Deut. 5:32–33; Isa. 30:19–26; John 15:12–17; Acts 13:1–2.

AN ACTION TO TAKE: Where can you find the courage to obey what God reveals in your prayerful study of His word?

A PRAYER TO MAKE: 'Lord, help me to be faithful in obeying all that You say to me, knowing that my obedience is an expression of Your mission on earth. Amen.'

Dare to be a Daniel by Philip P. Bliss (1873) hymntime.com [accessed 25/05/2021]

Luke 17:11–19

'One of them, when he saw he was healed, came back, praising God in a loud voice. He threw himself at Jesus' feet and thanked him – and he was a Samaritan.' (vv15–16)

The reaction of the leper who returned to thank Jesus is demonstrative; he 'threw himself at Jesus' feet'. This suggests a lot of energy, reflecting the scale of his gratitude. Someone, long placed beyond mainstream society, was cleansed and invited to become part of something precious from which he had been excluded. Reminiscent of the excitement we felt with the easing of lockdown in May and our freedom to see family and friends again, and even hug.

Jesus recalls that there were ten in the original leprous group, yet only one is aware of Jesus' work of healing and restoration. It's a stark reminder that we are to live our lives conscious of the grace we enjoy as followers of Jesus. This God awareness helps us to keep short accounts with God, and not to wander too far from God's presence, conscious of our dependence upon the love and life the Spirit of God gives us.

One reason we take time to unlock the Bible every day with Jesus is to nurture our God awareness. Only through obedience and attending to what God says through His word and in prayer can we successfully walk in Jesus' footsteps.

RELATED SCRIPTURE TO CONSIDER: Gen. 8:13–22; 2 Sam. 9; Luke 7:36–50; Col. 2:6–10.

AN ACTION TO TAKE: As you read Scripture, take time to become aware of what God is saying to you for today. God is alive and still speaks today.

A PRAYER TO MAKE: 'Lord, thank You for healing me from sin and its consequences. Teach me to return and give thanks to You often. Amen.'

1 Kings 8:14–21

**'The LORD has kept the promise he made: I have succeeded
David my father and now I sit on the throne of Israel, just
as the LORD promised, and I have built the temple for
the Name of the LORD, the God of Israel.'** (v20)

Solomon thanks God for three key foundations that sustain
Christian witness. First, he thanks God for his heritage. Next,
for his own calling and purpose and, finally, he declares God is
trustworthy.

Once a Christian, we become part of a family stretching back
throughout history (Rom. 11:16). Our bloodline is God's, and we join
Jesus' family (Heb. 2:11). Now we can look to a long line of faith-filled
women and men as our ancestors (Heb. 12:1).

The writer of Ecclesiastes makes clear that in many ways all is
meaningless (Eccl. 1:2). God's promise is that each one of us is called
according to God's purpose (Rom. 8:28–30); life is meaning-ful! Life only
makes sense through this Trinity-shaped lens. Solomon's father, David,
wanted to build a temple, yet this was not his God-given responsibility.
Each of us can rest in God's purpose for our life. Many of those family
members who have preceded us left an invisible legacy, yet one written
and recorded in God's book of life (Luke 10:20)

We also enjoy the assurance of safety in every moment of our life. For
we know that God is trustworthy and our lives are always safe in God's
hands (Psa. 139:16). We can therefore be at peace because we are
sustained by God's love today and every day.

RELATED SCRIPTURE TO CONSIDER: Psa. 139; Eccl. 1; Rom. 11:11–24; Heb. 2:5–18.

AN ACTION TO TAKE: Reflect on the lyrics of BeBe Winans: 'There's a time to
live and a time to die, so let's celebrate each moment of our life. And if we
ever lose our way, because the heart is torn, never let it question why's the
reason that we're born.''

A PRAYER TO MAKE: 'Lord, thank You for healing me from sin and its
consequences. Teach me to return and give thanks to You often. Amen.'

'*Born for This* by Bebe Winans (EMI; Blackwood Music Inc.; Benny's Music ©2002) musixmatch.com/lyrics/
BeBe-Winans-Stephanie-Mills/Born-for-This [accessed 26/05/2021]

John 6:5–13
'Jesus then took the loaves, gave thanks, and distributed to those who were seated as much as they wanted. He did the same with the fish.' (v11)

The reason for *Every Day with Jesus* is to unlock the Bible and open God's treasury of blessing contained within all of Scripture. It's taking the time to approach and settle down in front of Jesus, much as this crowd did on the mountainside. Then inviting Jesus to bless His Word and nourish us with fresh hope and new life.

Much like manna fell fresh from heaven every day to support Israel in the wilderness (Exod. 16:4), so we step aside to take time with God and find food for the day ahead of us. Equally, every day requires a fresh miracle of God's grace; yesterday's food cannot sustain us today. God's promise is to provide fresh nourishment each and every day.

Just as the Israelites had to get up and go out to collect the manna each morning, so we must go in search of God every day. There is a crisis of biblical literacy across the UK, a crisis Waverley Abbey is responding to with *EDWJ*. Literacy means not just reading God's Word but learning how to live God's Word every day. Waverley Abbey also runs practical courses online and face to face, to support people in how to live the Bible, whatever circumstances they find themselves in.

Scripture reminds us that without a vision the people perish (Prov. 29:18, KJV). Jesus is our vision, Scripture the source for our nourishment and our lives the witness to the enduring power of God's Word.

RELATED SCRIPTURE TO CONSIDER: Exod. 16:1–32; Psa. 107; 2 Tim. 3:14–17; Heb. 4:12–16.

AN ACTION TO TAKE: Come to Jesus every day and learn how to live Scripture. Introduce and help others to unlock the Bible with *EDWJ* **edwj.org/so21-24oct**

A PRAYER TO MAKE: 'Lord, open my eyes that I might see wonderful things in Your Word. Amen.' (Psa. 119:18)

Proverbs 30:7–9
**'Two things I ask of you, LORD; do not refuse me before I die:
keep falsehood and lies far from me; give me neither poverty
nor riches, but give me only my daily bread.'** (vv7–8)

Look around any church and you will observe great diversity. Whilst everyone seeks God, the range of experience is varied. From the financial wealth of individuals to their encounter with illness, from grief to joy, church offers a snapshot of individual life experience everywhere. One reason Paul reminds the church to rejoice with those who rejoice and weep with those who weep (Rom. 12:15).

The challenge with diversity is that it can provoke comparison. Yet, we are invited to build our confidence in following Jesus, not in comparing ourselves to others. Yes, as the body of Christ we make common cause with other disciples, and we invest our gifts for the benefit of the community. Such gifts include both skills and experience. The church community holds within it a deep wisdom born of life, wisdom that is a source of encouragement when appropriately shared throughout the community.

Within the community, we remain individuals learning to respond to God as He requires. Scripture does not present God's followers as a homogeneous bunch. Each is invited to live their own story under God's direction. Hence, the way God instructs one person to live their Christian witness is unique to that relationship. Indeed, the learning we gain as individuals is what enriches the whole and ensures the church is accessible to everyone, whatever their background and experience.

RELATED SCRIPTURE TO CONSIDER: Exod. 35:30–36:7; Josh. 1:1–11; John 21:15–23; Rom. 12.

AN ACTION TO TAKE: Redirect your interest and attention away from comparing yourself to others and ask God how He would like you to live your life serving Him.

A PRAYER TO MAKE: 'Lord, may I find my greatest fulfilment in knowing that I am living the life You have called me to. Amen.' (1 Cor. 7:17)

Little Christ

Proverbs 6:20–24
'My son, keep your father's command and do not forsake your mother's teaching. Bind them always on your heart; fasten them round your neck.' (vv20–21)

'**N**o one can have God as Father who does not have the church as Mother'. So said St Cyprian, whose quote is referred to by John Calvin throughout his *Institutes*.* This may sound a strange description, yet it is the Church that must submit to Christ in all things (Eph. 5:21–28). Indeed, the Church is the bride of Christ awaiting the glorious day when she will be united with Christ (Rev. 19:6–9).

If we want to know how to live a godly life, we have two teachers. The first is God speaking through Scripture. God's Word finds expression in the choices we take and the life we then live. C.S. Lewis describes the word Christian as 'little Christ', because we share in the life of Christ.** Perhaps more accurately, Christian means 'slave of Christ' (Rom. 6:22). Our behaviour is itself an expression of the truth and reality of God.

We are also called to be part of the Church. Here, the accumulated wisdom of all those disciples who have preceded us is held in trust on our behalf. In church, I am encouraged to worship and serve God. I find practical wisdom and support in navigating all life's challenges. I observe how others live out God's Word in their experience.

So, if I want to know how to live as a Christian, I look to two primary sources the Bible, God's living Word; and the Church, a present and organic body expressing God's life within a specific community. We do not need to work out how to follow Jesus in isolation. God has given us guides.

RELATED SCRIPTURE TO CONSIDER: Hosea 1; Matt. 25:1–13; 2 Cor. 11:1–4; Rev. 21:1–4.

AN ACTION TO TAKE: How does reading Scripture and interacting with church help you live your Christian life in practice?

A PRAYER TO MAKE: 'Lord, help me to live the life of God through obeying Your word and within Your Church. Amen.'

*Calvin's *Institutes of the Christian Religion* are available at ccel.org/ccel/calvin/institutes.toc.html
**C.S. Lewis, *Mere Christianity* (New York: Harper, 2009).

In Search of God

In the next edition of EDWJ we will find ourselves making our way to rediscover Jesus afresh in the crib at Bethlehem. Whilst Advent will particularly provide meditations on our Christmas journey, we shall take November and December to go in search of God.

Whether you are on a journey of exploration but have not as yet encountered the risen Christ, or have walked with Jesus for many years, it is good to renew our first love for the Redeemer of the world, and to prepare our hearts once again to welcome the incarnate Christ.

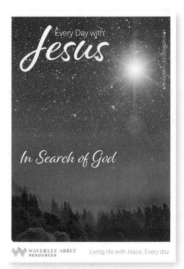

Also available as esubscription, ebook, audioversion and PDF.

Obtain your copy from **waverleyabbeyresources.org** or a Christian bookshop

Feast

Proverbs 15:13–18
'All the days of the oppressed are wretched, but the cheerful heart has a continual feast. Better a little with the fear of the LORD than great wealth with turmoil.' (vv15–16)

The consistent promise in the Bible is that fullness of life comes from God alone (Col. 2.9). This challenges human wisdom, and indeed Scripture tells the story of humanity's natural inconsistency, vacillating between following God and natural instinct.

Humanity's perennial search for contentment is uppermost in people's minds today. The relentless search for 'wellbeing' dominates public debate. Contentment means being happy with present conditions. Interestingly, many believe that changing the situation is the source of true happiness. In truth, it consists of changing one's attitude and approach to current circumstances.

Scripture reveals that this remains beyond our reach until, and unless, we find and make our peace with God. He has communicated fullness of life through Jesus, so peace is always available. We are the ones who must activate our experience of this peace through choosing to surrender to God.

Of course, the theory is all too easy to express; entering the experience of truth is altogether different. Yet this is what our mortal life is for, a school in discovering the presence of God in our life in every moment of every day. The question is, am I ready to go to school every day? How else might I grow in grace and learn to taste and see that the Lord is good (Psa. 34:8)?

RELATED SCRIPTURE TO CONSIDER: Psa. 34; Isa. 58:6–14; Matt. 6:25–34; 1 Cor. 7:17–24.

AN ACTION TO TAKE: No lesson is easy to master. Learning to practise the way of God every day is our challenge. Will we embrace it?

A PRAYER TO MAKE: 'Lord, teach me how to live fully in every circumstance of my life. Amen.'

Proverbs 16:1–11
**'In their hearts humans plan their course, but
the LORD establishes their steps.'** (v9)

To step is to take an action that leads to a result. God is interested in securing our safe encounter with Him. As we consider the many opportunities before us and the decisions we might take, we can never know what the results might be. We marry full of hope and anticipation, only to lose our partner suddenly to an unexpected illness. The child we longed for dies at birth and all our plans for our baby vanish.

Life often proves testing. We cannot find reasons for the tragedies we encounter. Unrealised dreams turn to ashes and our hearts may grow bitter. The very purpose for our lives can die with these dreams and we continue our life journey an empty shell, unable or unwilling to dream again.

At such times, God can appear both distant and uncaring. We desperately need to lay responsibility for our pain somewhere, and an all-powerful God who failed to intervene on our behalf appears fair game. Yet, what have we left once we have turned our back on God? We are alone, and no more capable of addressing our pain or explaining our circumstances.

Somewhere within that broken dream an ember of God's love and purpose still glows. Have we the courage to carry it in the hope it might once again relight the fire that once inspired our life? Can we ever recover hope from the wreckage that all too often litters our life experience?

RELATED SCRIPTURE TO CONSIDER: Psa. 69; 142; Isa. 40:27–31; Matt. 11:25–30; 19:24–30.

AN ACTION TO TAKE: Can you find the courage to carry the embers of hope when your plans literally collapse around you?

A PRAYER TO MAKE: 'Lord, save me, 'for the waters have come up to my neck. I sink in the miry depths, where there is no foothold'. Amen.' (Psa. 69:1–2)

Proverbs 18:20–21
**'From the fruit of their mouth a person's stomach is filled;
with the harvest of their lips they are satisfied.'** (v20)

Many of our emotions are accompanied by a physical experience. Grief grips the heart and constricts our breath. Often we act out the physical feeling we experience. We tense up with anger and give it physical or verbal expression.

Scripture is clear that we are a connected whole, and Paul states in Philippians, 'Their destiny is destruction, their god is their stomach, and their glory is in their shame. Their mind is set on earthly things' (Phil. 3:19). If we choose to live from our base emotions, we are going to find it very challenging to live every day with Jesus.

Just as the stomach is fed by our mouth, James reminds us that our mouths also give expression to what we have consumed from life's experience, 'With the tongue we praise our Lord and Father, and with it we curse human beings, who have been made in God's likeness' (James 3:9).

We can conclude that how we engage, or consume, life will have a significant impact on how we live our life. We take something from each experience and it feeds us physically, emotionally and spiritually. Therefore, we must set a guard over our mouths (Psa. 141:3).

Words expressed may impact our emotions. We start talking and find ourselves suddenly consumed with tears we weren't expecting. Scripture is clear: how we choose to manage ourselves in life's ups and downs has an impact on how consistently we live every day.

RELATED SCRIPTURE TO CONSIDER: Psa. 34:8–22; 141; Matt. 15:1–20; Eph. 4:25–32.

AN ACTION TO TAKE: Have you set a guard over your mouth so that only that which reflects God emerges from your lips?

A PRAYER TO MAKE: 'Lord, may I find the grace I need so that my words are sweeter than honey. Amen.' (Psa. 19:9–13)

Proverbs 27:19
'As water reflects the face, so one's life reflects the heart.' (v19)

O ur beliefs are what we hold to be true. As Christians, we choose to accept the saving grace of Jesus and the inspiration of Scripture. Whilst belief is easy to express in words, the test of our beliefs lies in the degree to which we express them through our life choices.

The beliefs we hold dear give us our values. Hence a Christian will accept as a core value the fact that Jesus taught to love one's neighbour as oneself. Such a belief, and the value it presents, can prove challenging when our attitude becomes involved in our internal conversation. There are other influences that shape our values.

Our life experiences will deeply influence our values, and can cause real interference as we wrestle with those beliefs God's Word requires us to embrace. Our behaviour can often be influenced by attitudes built from values as much as from belief.

In practice, this boils down to what we choose to lay as the foundation of our lives. Our actions stand as the greatest testimony to the beliefs that lie at the heart of who we are. It's why the heart is so central to all that Jesus taught.

Spiritual formation is the lifelong process we engage in whereby we attempt to establish attitudes and values that arise from God's Word, and our behaviour serves to reveal the reality of Christ. This is the testimony that counts, where our walk matches our talk.

RELATED SCRIPTURE TO CONSIDER: 2 Chron. 16:1–13; Matt. 7:21–29; 1 Tim. 3; Titus 2.

AN ACTION TO TAKE: What challenges do you face in living out your beliefs when your natural values and attitudes conflict?

A PRAYER TO MAKE: 'Lord, help me to be transformed from someone who lives by my values to someone who lives by Your values based on Scripture. Amen.'

Transformed

Proverbs 30:5–9
**'Keep falsehood and lies far from me; give me neither
poverty nor riches, but give me only my daily bread.'** (v8)

Learning to be satisfied with what one has is something Scripture encourages. It literally means to accept that what we have is enough. In a world where accumulation is the norm, it can prove difficult learning to be satisfied.

Yet in a world committed to accumulation, too often we find that some have far too much and others not simply enough. It can be argued that to be satisfied is the equivalent of lacking ambition. However, as disciples our ambition is to be transformed into a representation of God's kingdom.

Transformed means, 'to completely change the appearance or character of something or someone', usually for the better.* So, whilst I may remain physically recognisable with appearance never the focus for the transforming work of the Spirit how I react and initiate will be altogether different to how I behaved earlier in my life.

This is the transformational work of the Spirit; evident and quantifiable both by myself and by others. Our ambition is to become more like Jesus, with an ever-decreasing interest in what are secondary issues to God. Our wellbeing is realised as we grow to become more like Jesus day by day.

Our daily bread is being content with the knowledge that we are becoming more like Jesus, the inner transformation which is the true and lasting fruit of the gospel.

RELATED SCRIPTURE TO CONSIDER: Jer. 32:36–44; Ezek. 36:22–36; Phil. 4:10–20; Heb. 13:1–17.

AN ACTION TO TAKE: What robs you of living contentedly today? What action will you take in inviting God to transform you?

A PRAYER TO MAKE: 'Lord, thank You that I am a new creation in Christ and that the old has passed away and the new has come. Amen.' (2 Cor. 5:17)

Write to **micha@edwj.org** and I'll write back personally and in confidence as soon as I can.

Cambridge Dictionary, dictionary.cambridge.org/dictionary [accessed 30/05/2021]

Expectation and Wonder

Advent with Waverley Abbey Trust

Spark up the countdown as we reinvent adventing.
Join us for events to raise your wonder and build your
expectation. Dare to believe again this year.

Advent studies available

Journeying together through advent

waverleyabbeyresources.org/advent-2021

 C2C Advent: Journey to Christmas

 C2C Advent: Unexpected Jesus

 Advent Together

Notes